Ernst Heinrich Philipp August Haeckel

India and Ceylon

Ernst Heinrich Philipp August Haeckel

India and Ceylon

ISBN/EAN: 9783337246006

Printed in Europe, USA, Canada, Australia, Japan

Cover: Foto ©ninafisch / pixelio.de

More available books at **www.hansebooks.com**

INDIA AND CEYLON

INTRODUCTION.

 HEINRICH HAECKEL was born in Germany in
 is now a Professor of Zoology at the University of
He was among the first German writers to agree
rwin, and is one of the foremost leaders in that
of biologists, having published several works on
l themes in which he has advanced some interest-
ries of his own. For earnestness of study, and for
ible and lucid manner in which Prof. Haeckel ex-
is ideas, he ranks at the head of all the scientists
y.
 endeavored in the following pages to give a coherent
 if not strictly literal translation of Prof. Haeckel's
ng "Letters of Indian Travel," which appeared in
rm in the *Rundschau* (1882). Although the ter-
versed by the Professor is no *terra incognita* to most
 and many travelers, still he writes so enthusias-
d entertainingly about subjects which have here-
peared in merely scientific dress, statistics reports,
yclopædias, that I trust a version of them will be
le to the American reader.

TRANSLATOR.

INDIA AND CEYLON.

FROM THE GERMAN OF PROFESSOR ERNST HAECKEL.

TRANSLATED BY S. E. BOGGS.

I.

ON THE WAY TO INDIA.

"REALLY going to India?" questioned my friends in Jena; and, Really going to India, I repeated, I know not how often after I, at the close of the past winter, fully impressed with the melancholy dreariness of our North-German February, decided to spend the next winter in the tropical sunshine of that wonder-island Ceylon.

In this age of travel, when no part of our globe is spared by the adventuresome tourist, a voyage to India is no great feat. We speed across the most distant seas in the comfortable and luxurious steamships of the present, in less time, and with less ceremony and fewer accidents, than attended the dreaded journey to Italy a hundred years ago. Even a "tour around the world in eighty days" is become a familiar thought; and many inexperienced cosmopolitans, who possess the funds necessary for such a tour, imagine that it gives them a better, a more comprehensive "education," than they could obtain by ten years' hard study in our best schools.

With this fact in view, I can scarcely hope that my journey to India will arouse any particular interest—especially as an abundance of the best literature descriptive of that wonderful country is already in existence—and I ought perhaps to apologize for asking the reader to accompany me. My personal interests as naturalist and nature's friend alone prompt the journey I am about to undertake.

The most earnest desire of every naturalist that has made the organic forms of life a lifelong study, is to stand face to face with the wonders of nature in the tropics; for only here, under the enhancing influence of the sun's light and heat, are developed those astonishing types of form compared with which the flora and fauna of our temperate zone are but weak and colorless imitations.

Already as a boy, when poring over my favorite descriptions of travel, nothing charmed me so much as the primitive forests of India and Brazil; and later, when Humboldt's "Views of Nature," Schleiden's "Plant Life," and Darwin's "Voyage Around the World" influenced my plans for the future, a journey to the equatorial region became my chief desire. Believing that if I were a physician I might accomplish my purpose, I studied medicine in addition to botany and zoology; but a long period was to elapse before the realization of my cherished dream! The various attempts I made twenty-five years ago, after the termination of my medical studies, to accomplish the long-dreamed-of tropical journey were of no avail. I was fortunate enough, however, to spend a whole year on the shores of the Mediterranean, absorbed in studying the multifarious population of its waters.

Soon after my return from the Mediterranean certain professional duties, and an unexpected change in my private affairs, thrust all plans of travel into the remote background.

On Easter of 1861 I entered upon a professorship in the University of Jena, a position I have occupied for twenty years. During this time my vacations have been spent, in imitation of my distinguished master and friend Johannes Müller, in studying zoology along the seashores. An extraordinary predilection for the interesting study of the lower sea-animals—particularly the zoophytes and protozoans—gradually led me to visit every coast in Europe

INDIA AND CEYLON.

In the preface of my "System of the Medusæ" (1879) I have given a summary of the shores on which I fished, sketched, and made microscopic observations. But the diversified coast of the Mediterranean, whose attractions are, in many respects, far superior to any other place, always remained my favorite hunting ground.

I twice crossed the boundaries of my favorite territory. The winter of 1866–67 was spent among the Canary Islands, chiefly on Lanzarote, a volcanic island almost devoid of vegetation.

In the spring of 1873 I made a delightful excursion on an Egyptian war-ship, from Suez to Tur, of which I give an account in my "Arabian Corals" (1875). Both of these journeys took me to within a few degrees of the equatorial region—quite near enough to give me an idea of its exuberant vegetation.

The more a naturalist sees of our beautiful world the more desirous he becomes to enlarge his sphere of knowledge.

Shortly after my return from Genoa (1880)—where, thanks to Mr. Montague Brown, the English consul, I obtained many zoological and botanical treasures—chance threw into my hands Ransonnet's excellent work on Ceylon, and the tantalizing reminiscences of Portofino made the wonders of the Indian cinnamon-island appear all the more alluring. I consulted various route-books, and was rejoiced to find that the "struggle for existence" between the several Indian steamship lines had, naturally, reduced the high rates of passage, and had doubtless also abated many of the nuisances formerly attendant upon an Indian voyage. The announcement by the Austrian Lloyd Steamship Company that they now ran two lines of steamers to India (both touching at Ceylon) was of special interest to me. My numerous trips on the Mediterranean had very favorably impressed me with the Austrian Lloyd, and I at once concluded that through them I might at last attain my long-cherished wish. The voyage from Triest to Ceylon, by way of Aden, requires about four weeks. Six days are spent between Triest and Port Said, two days in the Suez Canal, six in the Red Sea, and eleven on the Indian Ocean between Aden and Ceylon. From three to four days are spent in touching at the different ports on the route. Accordingly a six months' leave of absence would allow two months for the voyage to and from India, and four months for travelling in Ceylon.

Circumstances which need not be here mentioned favoring an immediate decision, I began at once to prepare for the journey. Leave of absence was easily obtained, and a generous sum of money for the collection of natural curiosities was cheerfully granted by the Grand-ducal Government of Weimar.

In our day the naturalist who goes to the seashore to investigate marine plant and animal life, requires more than a microscope and the few simple instruments of twenty—nay ten years ago.

The methods for biological, and particularly microscopic research have wonderfully developed in the past decade, and a complicated apparatus is now considered indispensable for the performance of the simplest tasks. Consequently I was obliged to ship from Triest, sixteen chests and boxes. Two contained only the most necessary scientific works; two enclosed a microscope, physical and anatomical instruments; two others held the implements required for collecting, and the means for preserving, specimens of Indian flora and fauna. The remaining boxes contained several thousand vials, nets of all description, fishing-tackle, photographic camera, and the various articles I should require for sketching in oils and water-colors; a double-barrelled gun and ammunition, and lastly a supply of linen and clothing for a six months' journey.

In face of this imposing outfit, the preparing and packing of which caused me infinite worry and labor, I may consider myself rarely lucky in that not a single wish concerning my undertaking remained unfulfilled. It is a well-known fact that among all the investigations of marine life undertaken in late years, none have brought to light so many astonishing results as the deep-sea explorations of the English zoologists Sir Wyville Thomson, Messrs. Carpenter, Murray, Moseley, and others.

Twenty years ago it was believed that no life existed at the bottom of the ocean, that organic life ceased at a depth of two thousand feet; but the deep-sea investigations of the last ten years have substantially confuted this erroneous belief. That the ocean is densely populated to the depth of twenty-seven thousand feet with creatures of various species heretofore wholly unknown has been proved; and it has also been demonstrated that the different zones of the ocean are as abundantly supplied with diversified plant life as are the different flora-belts of the mountains.

The unequalled explorations of the *Challenger* expedition were confined chiefly to the Atlantic and parts of the Pacific oceans; the vast expanse of water comprising the Indian Ocean was not invaded, except at its most southerly boundary. Consequently an almost inconceivable wealth of new and wonderful creatures will doubtless reward the naturalist who first casts his perfected deep-sea net into the unexplored basin of the Indian Ocean.

Then was not I excusable if, while preparing for my journey to this unexplored region, I wished that I might be the one to discover hidden treasures? Even though the attempt proved abortive, it would still be the *first!*

But deep-sea explorations are a costly pleasure, even though they be conducted, as I proposed, in the simplest and most inexpensive manner. I could not think of undertaking such a project with my own private means, but I hoped to receive substantial support from those institutions which were founded solely for scientific purposes.

In this I was disappointed, and the initial investigation of the Indian Ocean remains to be made by a more fortunate explorer. For me it is to be hoped that the surface-water of that tropical sea will yield so much that is new and interesting that my brief holiday will be all too short for the full solution of its problems.

In contradistinction to this and some other far from agreeable experiences while preparing for my journey, I received the warmest encouragement and support from many valued friends, who, directly my plans were made known, sought in every way to further them. My heartiest thanks are due to Charles Darwin, Dr. Paul Rottenburg, of Glasgow; Sir Wyville Thomson, and John Murray, Esq., of Edinburgh. Also to Professor Edward Suess, of Vienna; Baron von Königsbrunn, of Gratz; Heinrich Krauseneck, and Captain Radonetz, of Triest.

My special gratitude is due to his royal highness the Grand Duke Carl Alexander of Saxe-Weimar, the *Rector*

Magnificentissimus of the Jena University, and to the hereditary grand duke, through whose kindly agency I received letters of introduction from the English Colonial Minister to the governor of Ceylon.

My arrangements at last completed, and the sixteen boxes sent in advance to Triest, I was ready to take leave of dear quiet Jena on the morning of the 8th of October. When the last moment arrived, I found that a six months' absence from home would be no easy task for the father of a family who had already attained the age of forty-eight years. With what different emotions would I have taken my departure twenty-five years ago, when a tropical journey was the chief aim of my life! True, the experience of twenty-five years of teaching and zoological study would enable me to accomplish more than I could have done a quarter of a century ago. But I was twenty-five years older. Would the concrete wonders of tropical nature possess the same fascination for me now that I had penetrated the abstract dominions of natural philosophy?

These and kindred thoughts, together with the most doleful impressions of my last farewells to home and friends, passed through my brain as the train bore me through the cold gray autumnal mists which enshrouded my beloved Saale valley.

Only the tallest peaks of our magnificent *muschelkalk* mountains rose above the misty sea; on the right, Hausberg with his "rosy radiant summit," the proud pyramid of the Jenzig, and the romantic ruins of Kunitzburg. On the left stretched the wooded heights of Rauthal; and, further on, Goethe's favorite retreat, charming Dornburg. I waved an adieu to these dear old mountain friends, and promised to return to them in good health, and richly laden with Indian treasures.

As if to ratify the promise they gave me their friendliest morning greeting: the dense fog suddenly fell from their shoulders, and the triumphant sun rose into a perfectly cloudless sky. Thousands of dewdrops blazed like jewels in the azure cups of the lovely gentians decorating the grassy slopes on either side of the iron road.

I took advantage of the several hours' halt in Leipzig to make some necessary additions to my travelling equipments, and to enjoy a brief view of the noble masterpieces in the public picture gallery.

Then on to Dresden and Vienna.

After a brief halt in the latter city I continued my journey to Gratz. It was a glorious sunshiny Sunday, and the alpine beauties of the Semmering glowed with splendor. It was twenty years ago when I botanized in the woody ravines and flower-adorned alp-farms of romantic Steiermark, but every nook on the Schneeberg and the Rax-Alp is still remembered with pleasure. In those days the youthful *Doctor Medicinae* was more devoted to the interesting flora and fauna of the mountains, than to the instructive clinics of Oppolzer and Skoda, Hebra and Siegmund; and often, while gathering the hardy alpine plants, dreamed of the luxuriant vegetation of the tropics he was now so soon to see.

I spent a day in Gratz, where I found really excellent accommodations at the "Elephant Hotel." Could a more appropriate name have been found for the first hostelry in which I lodged on my way to India? The elephant, aside from his eminent position as one of the most important animals, is conspicuous in the armorial bearings of Ceylon, and I accepted the hospitable treatment of the Gratz elephant as a favorable prognostic of the acquaintance I hoped soon to make with his Indian brother. Just here I shall take the opportunity to insert an observation made for the benefit of my travel-loving fellows, especially for those that care less for the number of black-coated waiters at a hotel than for attentive service from them.

A long and varied experience with hotels of all grades has taught me that the traveller may, to a certain extent, judge the state and condition of these useful institutions by the titles they bear. I have divided them into three classes: the zoological-botanic, the dubious, and the dynastic. I have found that by far the best of the three is the zoological-botanic, as, for instance, the "Golden Lion," "White Horse," "Silver Swan," "Green Tree," "Golden Vine," etc. You cannot be certain of good and cheap accommodations in the houses which I have classified as dubious, and which have no affinity with either the first or the third group; they bear various names (frequently that of the proprietor himself), and are of too heterogeneous a character for a definite generalization. I have had chiefly doleful experiences—high prices and inferior accommodations—with the dynastic class, such as the "Emperor of Russia," "King of Spain," etc. Of course, by this classification I do not presume to establish a general rule, but, on the whole, I believe that the critical and unpretending wanderer will find that I am right. The "Elephant" in Gratz substantiated its claim to an honorable place in the zoological-botanic class.

Baron von Königsbrunn, a distinguished landscape painter in Gratz, who had heard of my proposed journey to Ceylon, cordially invited me to inspect the sketches he had made while on that island in 1853. The baron travelled through the palm forests and fern ravines of the cinnamon island in company with Ritter von Friedau and Professor Schmarda of Vienna, the latter of whom has given a comprehensive description of the island in his "Tour Around the World." Unfortunately the sketches which Baron von Königsbrunn made, and which were originally intended to illustrate Professor Schmarda's work, were never published, a fact to be regretted, as they are the best and the most perfect of the kind I have yet seen. Alexander von Humboldt, certainly a competent judge, who submitted the views to the inspection of King Friederich Wilhelm IV., expressed for them his highest praise.

These paintings, which illustrate Ceylon vegetation and scenery, possess two different—and, in a measure, opposing—qualities, which are rarely found in like works of art. They are, a conscientious adherence to nature in the reproduction of details, and an artistic freedom in the individual treatment and effective composition of the whole picture. Many of the landscapes by our most celebrated artists possess the second, but do not even suggest the first quality; while, on the other hand, in many of the so-called views of vegetation, by practical botanists, the absence of æsthetic perception is only too obvious. For a perfect picture, the synthetic and subjective glance of the artist is as necessary as the analytic and objective eye of the naturalist; in other words, the perfect landscape must, like the portrait, unite striking resemblance to the subject with artistic perception of individual characteristics, and this attribute Königsbrunn's sketches possess to a wonderful degree. I take this occasion to express my sincere thanks to the modest as well as gifted and original artist, and hope that his charming works of art may soon find their way from the obscurity of his studio to a deservedly prominent place in public.

On the 11th of October I bade adieu to the multitude of old and new friends in Gratz, and continued my journey on the Southern Railway to Triest. In the same compartment with me was an elderly gentleman whom at a first glance I recognized as English, and our first half-hour's conversation revealed a very interesting personage. It was Surgeon-general J. Macbeth, who had spent thirty-three years in India, in the service of his mother country. He had taken active part in a number of battles; had travelled throughout India, from Afghanistan to Malacca; had ascended the Himalaya Mountains, and travelled in Ceylon. His varied experiences on land and among different peoples, as well as his observations as physician and naturalist, were, as you may imagine, highly interesting and instructive, and I was almost sorry when our arrival at Triest near midnight concluded a most enjoyable conversation.

The three days I was compelled to wait in Triest for the sailing of the Austrian Lloyd steamer were passed in the society of old friends, whose hospitable treatment made the hours pass so quickly that no time was left for a visit to poetic Miramare, that enchanting castle by the sea, whose natural beauties eminently fit it for an act in the tragedy of " Maximilian, Emperor of Mexico," a promising subject for the dramatist of the future.

Nor was I able to make an excursion to Muggia Bay, the body of water so rich in sea animals, which became famous through Johannes Müller's discovery of the curious snail (*Entoconcha mirabilis*) which lives in the sea-cucumber (Holothure). Aware that the Austrian Lloyd Company had frequently accorded special privileges to scientific travellers, I hoped to obtain similar favors. I was successful beyond my expectations, and here express my gratitude to the manager of the line, Baron Marco di Morpurgo, and to the directors, among whom is my esteemed friend Captain Radonetz.

And now to embark!

I had my choice between the two splendid ships which

sailed at the same time (15th October). The *Helios* touched at Aden, Bombay—where she remained eight days—Ceylon, Singapore, and Hong Kong. The *Polluce* touched at Jedda (the famous port of Mecca), Aden, Ceylon, and Calcutta. I chose the former vessel, which would give me a chance to visit Bombay and obtain a view of the Indian peninsula. Besides, the *Helios*, which was the better, faster, and larger of the two ships, was almost new, and of very attractive appearance. In addition to this, the name had a peculiar fascination for me. Could a more auspicious title than that of the ever-young sun-god be found for the vessel which was to bear me from the gray fog-regions of the north to the radiant sunshine and palm forests of the tropics?

Nomen et omen! Why might not I as well as my neighbor cherish a little superstition? Surely I might reckon on the favor of the sun-god, in whose honor I named a whole class of dainty protozoans, *Heliozoa*, *i.e.*, sun-animals! Therefore, most worthy *Helios*, let this zoological oblation kindly dispose you towards an admiring mortal, and safely bring him to the haven where he would be!

The very first days of the voyage proved that the gait of our *Helios* was a capital one. Although the sea was pretty rough there was comparatively little motion. Especially pleasant was the unusual neatness of everything about the vessel; there were no offensive odors from the kitchen and engine room—odors which contribute more towards seasickness than the rolling and pitching of the ship. Consequently I, and most of the passengers, escaped being seasick. The weather was uninterruptedly clear, and the sea generally smooth. Of all the voyages I have made, the one on the *Helios* was by far the pleasantest. Of course the agreeable company on board, and my cordial relations with the ship's officers, did much towards making it so.

The larger half of our company was composed of English army officers, government officials, and merchants. The other half was made up of Germans, Austrians, Bombay merchants, and a few missionaries. There was but a meagre representation of the fair sex: only one German and five English ladies. My amiable country-woman, who sang and played on the piano, contributed not a little towards the entertainment of her fellow-passengers. She had spent the summer with her children in Frankfort, and was returning to her husband in Bombay—a semi-annual separation between husband and wife practised by so many German and English residents of India who are solicitous about the education and morals of their children. As is generally the case on a voyage of considerable duration, the passengers on the *Helios* became pretty well acquainted with each other, and formed themselves into little *coteries*. One group was formed by the missionaries, among whom was a Mr. Rowe, an American, who has written a very readable book on "Every-day Life in India;" a second group was composed of the English officers and merchants; a third comprised the Germans and Austrians, the ship's captain and doctor, and myself.

As I have said before, the weather during the entire voyage continued uniformly fair; the sky was serene and cloudless; the sea smooth, or only gently undulating. Our good ship made every one of her ports at the appointed time; the victims of the demon seasickness were but few.

This uninterrupted sameness at length became monotonous. Reading, writing, cards, chess, music, vocal and instrumental, everything that is usually practised to relieve the tedium of a long voyage, had been exhausted the first week out. Consequently the five periods into which the day was divided by as many meal-times grew to be of more importance as the journey progressed. Unfortunately for me my poor German-professor's stomach is so very capricious on shipboard that—although I am rarely seasick— I always lose my appetite, while that of my fellow-passengers seems to increase in inverse ratio as mine diminishes. However, this condition of affairs enables me—as objective spectator—to observe the colossal capacity for what physiologists term the "consumption of luxuries." I have ever cherished a secret admiration for our able cousins across the Channel, whose gastronomic feats far surpass our own; but what I saw accomplished by an English major on board the *Helios* exceeded anything of the kind I ever beheld! This brave warrior enjoyed not only the five regular meals, with a liberal accompaniment of wine and beer, but most ingeniously managed to dispose of all manner of toothsome sweets and various beverages during the intervening periods. To me this gastronomic wonder seemed to have arrived at that state of development in which the perfected digestive organs are capable of constant activity, and I am strongly tempted to believe this activity was continued throughout the night, for I frequently saw the major stagger from his cabin at unconscionably early hours.

I have heard that the greater number of English residents in India who die from diseases contracted in that country invite their fate by excessive indulgence of the appetite.

As the meals on board an India-bound steamer are famous affairs—of vital importance indeed to some of the passengers—I may as well give the curious reader an idea as to what composes them. Coffee and bread are served at eight o'clock in the morning; at ten follows a general breakfast, at which appear eggs, meats, curry and rice, vegetables and fruits. At one o'clock "tiffin"—which is a luncheon of cold meats, bread and butter, potatoes, and tea. At five o'clock the regular dinner is served: soup, meats, with attendant relishes, farinaceous dishes, dessert, fruits, and coffee. Lastly, at eight o'clock in the evening a meal of tea, bread and butter, etc., concludes the list.

Very few of the passengers fail to make their appearance in the dining-saloon at the appointed hours. After meals the passengers promenade the deck, or recline in comfortable Chinese chairs, and discuss the never-changing tint of the azure sky and water.

An ever-welcome incentive to increased mental activity are the different marine creatures which occasionally appear: dolphins disporting around the vessel, gulls and petrels encircling gracefully overhead, or darting down upon their finny prey. Sometimes swarms of flying-fish skim swiftly across the crests of the waves. The delicate medusæ always charmed me most, and I was only sorry that the swift course of the vessel prevented me from securing some of these beautiful animals. In the Mediterranean Ocean, which is especially rich in sea-nettles, I saw two mammoth specimens: a blue *Pilema pulmo*, and a golden-brown *Cotylorhiza tuberculata*, and in the Indian Ocean a rose-colored *Aurelia*, and a dark-red *Pelagia*.

The voyage from Triest to Bombay (twenty-four days) was accomplished under such favorable conditions that there is scarcely anything of interest to chronicle. My former voyages in the blue Adriatic were chiefly along the picturesque shores of Istria and Dalmatia, the rosemary-scented islands of Lissa and Lesina, on the latter of which, in 1871, I spent a very pleasant month in the Franciscan monastery with the eminent Padre Buona Grazia.

This time our course was more toward the west—toward the middle of the Adriatic, as we were to land for several passengers at Brindisi. Above the heights of Canossa hung a black cloud, the shadow, perhaps, of—but I will not introduce politics here!

On the morning of the 17th (October) we landed at Brindisi. As we were to remain until noon I went ashore to view the few unimportant remains of ancient Brundusium, and wandered along the ramparts to the railway station. This structure, as well as the modern city itself, is not what one would naturally expect from the ostentatious title the latter assumed at the opening of the Suez Canal: the "entrepôt for the commerce of the world."

The overland mail is transferred to the steamer immediately after the arrival of the mail train, and the passengers—those going to and those returning from India—make the change from the cars to the steamer or *vice versa* with equal celerity, seeming in no way disposed to rest or refresh themselves in the only hotel in the place.

Both hotel and railway station were deserted the morning I was there; and not a soul was to be seen except the telegraph operator and a station porter. The flat coast with its vegetable gardens, plantations of reeds, and scattered date-palms, is very uninteresting. An old cathedral with a stately dome south of the city is the only object worth transferring to the sketch-book.

The English general whom, with his family and retinue, we were to have taken on board, did not make his appearance—his luggage having failed to arrive with him on the train—so we set sail again at noon without him. The following morning we steamed past the Ionian Islands; with pleasure I hailed the sight of stately Cephalonia, and greeted proud Monte Nero, on whose snow-clad height I once spent a memorable day in the shadow of a majestic *Pinus Cephalonica*—a noble evergreen found only on this island. Farther on we passed romantic Zante—"Fior di Levante"

—sailing so close to its southern shore that we could plainly see the long rows of vaulted grottoes and eaves in the red marble cliffs. In the afternoon Epirus appeared on our left, and on our right the solitary island of Stamphania. Late in the evening we passed battle-stained Navarino; no less attractive and picturesque was the view of Candia, whose southern coast we skirted on the 19th.

Fleecy clouds, scudding before a fresh breeze across the deep blue sky, cast fleeting shadows on the rugged bosom of the island, and occasionally enveloped Mount Ida's snow-crowned head. The next morning there was nothing but water on every side; but the increasing warmth of the temperature, which made us change our heavy clothing for lighter summer attire, apprised us of the nearness of the African coast.

When we went on deck on the morning of the 21st the Egyptian shores were not yet in sight, but the water of the Mediterranean had lost its incomparable azure tint, and was of a greenish hue that, as the ship progressed, gradually changed to a dirty greenish-yellow—the effect of the muddy waters of the Nile. And now appeared numbers of tiny sailing craft, principally Arabian fishing-boats. A huge sea-turtle drifted past the vessel; several land-birds flew on board, and at twelve o'clock noon we sighted the light tower of Damietta. At four o'clock a small steam launch brought a pilot to the *Helios*, and an hour later we cast anchor in the harbor of Port Said, which is at the northern entrance of the Suez Canal. The *Helios* remained here a day to take in coal and provisions. In the evening I and a number of the passengers went ashore to a *café*, where we met the doctor of the *Polluce* and several of her passengers —that ship having arrived at the same time with the *Helios*.

The following morning I mounted to the top of the light-tower, which is 160 feet high—the tallest in the world. Its electric light is seen at a distance of twenty-one nautical miles. The massive walls of the tower are built of the same material as that in the moles of the harbor—an artificial stone which is composed of two parts sand and one part hydraulic lime. The view from the tower did not come up with my expectations, as, with the exception of the town itself, and the flat stretches of sand surrounding it, nothing but water is to be seen.

I next visited the costly piers, which were constructed, at an enormous outlay of money and labor, to protect the entrance of the canal from its two principal enemies: the mud from the mouths of the Nile, and the sand from the desert. The western mole has a length of 3000 metres, and is considerably stronger than the one on the east, which is only half as long. For the construction of these moles 30,000 blocks of stone—each of 10 cubic metres, and 20,000 kilograms weight,—were required.

From the harbor I sauntered to the Arabian part of the town which is separated from European Port Said by a stretch of sandy desert; both quarters consist of parallel rows of streets which cross each other at right angles. The motley and original scenes in the filthy streets were the same one sees in every smaller Egyptian city, and in the suburbs of Cairo and Alexandria.

The European quarter is composed chiefly of shops and stores, and has perhaps 10,000 inhabitants. The expectations of grandeur entertained by the founders of Port Said have been only partially realized, and the imposing "Netherland hotel" already wears an air of solitude and desertion. I purchased a number of articles, considered indispensable by the voyager to India; among them a white broad-brimmed *solà* hat, and a comfortable bamboo extension-chair.

So much has been written about the Suez Canal—the wonder of modern times—that I shall not weary the reader by repeating well-known facts. We passed through the greater part of the canal on Sunday (23d). The morning in Menzaleh Lake was delightfully fresh and clear; thousands of pelicans, flamingoes, herons, and other aquatic fowl literally covered the sand-banks with which the lake is interspersed. After crossing Abu Ballah Lake we entered the narrowest part of the canal at El Guisr, where occurs the deepest cutting in the whole line. The high walls of sandy soil on either side are studded here and there with gray tamarisk shrubs; swarms of Arab children appear along the banks and clamor for *backshish*. Several boys play the flute and dance with considerable grace. At noon we passed Ismalia, the deserted city founded by De Lesseps, and in the evening we anchored in the Bitter Lakes.

Travellers to India dread the voyage through the Red Sea, it being the hottest and most disagreeable part of the route. Although it was the cooler season of the year we on the *Helios* were fully convinced that the dread aforementioned was well founded. But two thirds of the Red Sea, or Arabian Gulf, are within the torrid zone, yet the entire expanse of water composing it might well be called a tropical sea. Similar physical peculiarities characterize its shore from Suez to Perim—from 30°–13° N. Lat. Indeed the dissimilarity between its northern and southern extremities, removed from each other by a distance of three hundred miles—is much less than the difference between the Red Sea at Suez and the Mediterranean at Port Said, although the two localities are separated by but a narrow isthmus. But this bridge of land, which is the connecting link between Asia and Africa, has existed for millions of years, consequently the animal and vegetable population of the neighboring seas have developed perfectly independent of each other. Those along the Mediterranean shore belong to the Atlantic Ocean, while those of the Red Sea country are allied to the flora and fauna of the Indian Ocean. Both shores of the Red Sea, the eastern coast of Arabia, as well as the western coast of Egypt, are almost devoid of vegetation; not a single large river flows from them into the sea. Above the sterile shores, on either side, tower lofty mountain chains whose aspect is of the most forbidding character. Between these ranges, which glow with the intense heat from the sun, the narrow Arabian Gulf lies like a trench between two high walls; here, during the hot summer months, the mercury rises—in the shade at noon—to 40° R.! I was assured by the officers of the *Helios*, who had made the voyage during these periods, that this terrible heat was almost intolerable, and that often they had been afraid reason would desert them. Even yet, at the end of October, the heat was intense. The thermometer, which hung in a shady corner on deck, registered from 22°–26° R., and once in the "airy" cabins the mercury rose during the day to 32°, and at night it stood at 26°. The little air that stirred was oppressive, and every attempt to mitigate the intense heat proved unavailing. Every window, every hatchway, was left open day and night; two rows of ventilating chimneys conducted air into the hold of the vessel; the punkas in the saloons were kept constantly in motion. The air from these huge fans, together with an unlimited supply of ice water, alone enabled us to endure the excessive heat.

At seven o'clock on the morning of the 27th we crossed the Tropic of Cancer, and I breathed, for the first time, the fervid atmosphere of the torrid zone. The sky directly above us was perfectly clear, but away in the east, above the Arabian coast, loomed dense masses of storm-clouds that were illumined every second by flashes of heat lightning. There was a repetition of this cloud-picture in the eastern sky every evening, but no rain-storm came to refresh us. The first three nights in the tropics, the mercury never once fell below 25° in the cabins. I, as well as most of the gentlemen, slept on deck, where it was at least three degrees cooler.

On the night of the 30th we passed the straits of Babèl-Mandeb, and the island of Perim—the Gibraltar of the Red Sea—and on the morning of the 31st we anchored in the Gulf of Aden. Aden, as you know, is situated on a rocky peninsula, that, like Gibraltar, is connected with the mainland by a narrow neck of land. In 1839 it fell into the hands of the English, who fortified it, and made it an important station on the route to India. It has a population of 3000 souls. Most of the ships stop at Aden for coal and provisions; but, as the cholera had been raging there for two months, and we were not certain whether we would be allowed to land, we had taken in supplies at Port Said. However, on landing we found that the epidemic had shortly before entirely disappeared. The *Helios* was immediately surrounded by boats, and all sorts of peculiar wares were offered for sale by the dusky natives—ostrich feathers and eggs; lion and leopard skins; antelope horns; formidable saws of the saw-fish; dainty little baskets and trays, etc., etc. I was more attracted by the venders of these articles; there were genuine Arabs, negroes, Somalis, and Abyssinians. Most of them were of a dark-brown color, that, in some shaded into a reddish bronze, and in others to the deepest black. Some of them had their hair dyed red with henna, or bleached white with lime; and the greater number wore only a white cloth around the loins. We were greatly entertained by the swarms of dusky children—from eight to ten years old—who rowed out to the ship in tiny canoes made of hollow logs, and darted into the water head-foremost for the coins flung to them by the passengers. As we did not go ashore we saw but little of the town and its fortifications. The volcanic rocks on which the houses are scattered are rather picturesque. The prevailing color of the naked walls of lava is a dark brown that is here and there relieved by the dingy green of a few scant shrubs. In midsummer, life on this glowing pile of rock must be, for the English garrison, almost unendurable; and the officers are justified in naming the place the "Devil's Punch-bowl."

After a six hours' delay at this inhospitable port we set sail again for Bombay. Nothing of special interest occurred during the eight days' voyage across the Indian Ocean. The autumn weather was delightful; that we were in the influence of the north-east monsoon became daily more perceptible. Although the mercury still lingered in the neighborhood of $20°$ R., a fresh breeze mitigated the heat during the day, while the cool nights convinced us that we were beyond the oppressive influence of the Red Sea. The water, broken into ripples by the fresh wind, was constantly in motion; its color was a delicate blue-green—at times the tint of *lapis-lazuli*, but never the intense blue of the Mediterranean. Sometimes the sky would be perfectly clear; then again fleecy clouds would entirely obscure it. Every afternoon dense cloud-masses gathered along the horizon in the north-east and south-west, and these the setting sun would transform into the most gorgeous spectacle—an ever-new, ever-changing panorama that vanished all too quickly from our admiring gaze.

I stood for hours at the prow and watched the myriads of flying-fish that darted from the waves at the approach of the vessel. But more attractive always were the medusæ, of which we passed scores, blue rhizostomes, rose-colored aurelias, and red-brown pelagias. I particularly regret my failure to secure a remarkable siphonophora—of the species we call Porpita—that passed us on the 4th of November.

II.
A Week in Bombay.

A GLORIOUS and memorable day for me was the 8th of November. On that day I first set foot on tropical earth, and looked with astonishment on its animal and vegetable wonders.

A whole hour before sunrise I went on deck, and beheld advancing through the mists of dawn the deeply-dented coast of Bombay, above and beyond which rises that singular range of mountains, the "Bhor-Ghaut."

These mountains, which form the boundary wall between the extensive table-land of the Deccan, and the flat, narrow coast of Concan, the littoral lowlands of the Indian peninsula, are composed of plutonic basalt, syenite, and other rocks, and are so cloven and crenelated that one almost believes one is looking at colossal fortresses, pagodas, and battlements.

The morning sky was tinted with delicate evanescent hues which suddenly vanished altogether when, from between two broad belts of vapor, the splendid Indian *Helios* came forth to greet his gallant namesake from the north. And now the physical details of the approaching shore were clearly revealed; the most prominent features are the extensive groves of Palmyra palms, and the magnificent harbor, in which thousands of ships may safely ride at anchor. Of the city itself we could see only the detached houses of the Colaba quarter on the south-eastern point of the island, the imposing masonry of the stately fortress, and, in the distance, the verdant crest of Malabar Hill. with its numerous villas and gardens. The tumult and bustle among the shipping in the roomy harbor was very interesting. Before us lay two white ironclad monitors, with revolving turrets, most efficient defenders of the tropical city. Farther on we passed two large transports, on which were hundreds of English soldiers; and still farther on we wended our way through whole fleets of steamers that fetch and carry freight and passengers from every nation under the sun.

Shortly after sunrise the *Helios* anchored near the "Apollo-bunder," the place of debarkation; sanitary and customs officials came on board, and very soon the company that, for twenty-four days, had occupied the swimming hotel, dispersed in all directions. Hurried farewells were spoken, cards and good wishes exchanged, then each one made all possible haste to reach the long-wished-for *terra firma*. I was invited by a hospitable countryman of mine, Herr Blaschek, the husband of the German lady on the *Helios*, to spend the week of my sojourn in Bombay with him on Malabar Hill. Knowing well how the traveller's freedom of movement is restricted by the disagreeable boarding-school constraint of the English hotels in India, I gladly accepted Herr Blaschek's invitation; and, although I was surrounded by unusual splendor and magnificence—indispensable necessaries to the wealthy European in India, but rare luxuries to the modest German traveller—I soon felt perfectly at home among the palms and bananas of Blaschek villa.

It is of course impossible to become thoroughly acquainted with a place like Bombay in one short week; I shall not, therefore, attempt a detailed account of its numerous attractions. I had read and heard very little more about Bombay than that it was, after Calcutta, the largest and most important city of British India; that its commercial reputation was world-wide, and that it had a mixed population. I never saw in any of our art exhibitions views of this city or of its surroundings; imagine then my surprise when I found here sights which, for beauty and grandeur, can be compared only with those of Naples or Cairo—or, better, a peculiar combination of those two widely-dissimilar cities. Bombay is like Naples in its charming situation on an undulating and verdure-clad shore, its insular appendages, and its mountains. It is like Cairo, in that it contains a motley and picturesque population, representatives of every clime and race, and in the intense hues both nature and art have given their multifarious creations.

The city of Bombay is situated on an island which has an area of twenty-two square miles; it lies in lat. 18° 56' long., 72° N. 56' W. The island was first discovered and taken possession of by the Portuguese in 1529, who called it *Buona Bahia* (Good Bay), because of the large and excellent harbor which encloses it and the several adjacent islands. (It is also said that Bombay is derived from Bomba-Devi, the name of the Indian goddess of the sea.)

In 1661 the Portuguese ceded Bombay Island to the English, who at first scarcely knew what to do with their new possession. Its development was hindered chiefly by the extensive marshes which covered its surface, and which were supposed to render the climate unhealthy. When these swamps were drained, and other improved conditions established, the island rapidly developed—especially since 1820, when Mountstuart Elphinstone assumed the reins of government—and in the last fifty years Bombay has become the third largest commercial city in Asia.

Its present population is perhaps 800,000 (including 8000 Europeans and 50,000 Parsees). In 1834 there were but 234,000 inhabitants; in 1816, 160,000, and in 1716, only 16,000 souls.

Bombay, through her position as medium for the entire trade and commerce of the Indian Orient, and as connecting link between Asia and Europe, has again attained the prominence which was hers in the time of her greatest prosperity, the antiquity of Alexandria. Her most important traffic is cotton, in which she is surpassed only by New Orleans, in North America.

The immense harbor, as secure as it is extensive, is the largest and best in India. It opens towards the south, is bounded on the north by the mainland, on the west by Bombay Island, and on the north by a group of smaller islands. The island is rectangular in shape, and extends north and south; bridges connect its northern extremity with the island of Salsette, and the mainland. The greater portion of the northern half is covered by the extensive palm-forests of Mahim. The southern half consists of two long promontories, which are said to resemble the uneven claws of a crab, and which enclose the broad expanse of water known as Back Bay.

Of these two tongues of land, the western, which is the shorter and the higher—it is very like the Posilippo, near Naples—is Malabar Hill, the delightful villa quarter of Bombay. Beautiful gardens ornamented with luxuriant tropical plants surround the numerous elegant villas or bungalows which are the homes of the more distinguished residents of Bombay. On the eastern tongue of land is the suburb of Colaba, which contains the cotton market and the tents and barracks of the English soldiers. At the northern extremity of Colaba, between it and the fort, is the Apollo bunder, the handsome quay, on which the traveller to the Orient first sets foot. The name of this landing-place is not derived from that of the beautiful Greek god, but from *pallow* (fish), which eventually became Apollo. Pallow-bunder is Indian for fish-market. There is an excellent hotel on the quay, the only large and first-class hotel in Bombay, and here, on the balcony, in full view of the harbor and mountains, I enjoyed my first breakfast in India. On the esplanade of the Apollo-bunder, as on the Santa Lucia at Naples, the greatest activity prevails, especially in the evening, when the military band adds music to the attractions of the place, and the wealth and fashion of Bombay appears. Numbers of elegant equipages roll along the bay shore, while the native population amuses itself in its own peculiar manner around the bonfires on the strand. That portion of the island between Malabar Hill and Colaba, is occupied by the two most important sections of the city the "Fort," and the "Black Town." The former encloses the greater part of the European quarter, in which are to be found most of the public buildings, as well as most of the counting-houses and offices of the European residents.

Most of the public buildings, which were erected at an enormous expense in the last twenty or thirty years, are imposing structures, with the Gothic arches and peristyles of the Venetian palaces, architectural characteristics that are strangely at variance with the wanton luxuriance of the tropical vegetation around them, and the motley current of Indian life surging at their portals. The proper theatre, however, for scenes of Indian life is in the Black Town—the quarter inhabited by the native population. When I first visited this part of Bombay I was vividly reminded of Cairo. The public display of Oriental wares in the crowded bazaars, the cries of the venders, the gay costumes or half-naked forms of the surging throng in the narrow streets, the tumult of vehicles and horses—all these are like what you may see in the business quarters of Cairo. But the longer you are surrounded by the turmoil of this Indian city the more apparent becomes the difference between it and the cities of Egypt. The north-western portion of the Black Town (which is called Girgaum) is of a more pleasing aspect; here, in the shade of graceful cocoa-palms, are picturesque native huts, which, with the nude children playing around them, the gayly-dressed women and dusky men, pretty zebus, horses, dogs, monkeys, etc., offer a variety of the most enchanting sujects to the *genre* painter.

To adequately describe the diverse manners and customs of Bombay's heterogeneous population passes the power of my pen. The Hindus, who form the largest section, are of rather diminutive stature, delicate build, and dark brown color. The Hindu children are most charming; their little naked forms are to be seen everywhere. Even the adult males of the lower classes wear only a narrow scarf around the loins; consequently the artist or sculptor might here with advantage study the structure of the human form, the youths of sixteen to twenty years offering specially fine models. Indeed, one might justly call these shapely lads the "fairer sex;" their features are often refined and noble, and distinguished by a dreamy expression that is very attractive. There are also some neat figures among the women, whose simple flowing garments give them an exceedingly graceful appearance, but a really handsome feminine face is rare. The girls marry very young—at ten or fifteen years of age; they fade quickly and become extremely ugly old women. In addition to their natural homeliness they disfigure their faces by wearing in the left nostril a silver hoop adorned with precious stones, and many of these nose-rings are so large that the mouth and chin are covered by them. The women also chew betel, which stains the lips and teeth a vivid yellow. The forehead is striped with various colors to indicate the caste of the wearer, the arms are tattooed, and both sexes wear silver bangles and rings around the ankles and toes. In this garb the Hindu, although, he is descended from the same race—the Aryan—as that of our European forefathers, appears a genuine "savage." Caste distinctions and the Brahminical faith prevail among them to this day; the Hindu still burns the bodies of his dead, and, when riding along the shore of Back Bay, you may see in the immediate vicinity of the railway station the huge ovens in which by the simplest process the dead bodies are transformed to ashes—a more convenient and less costly method of cremation than is at present practised in Gotha. According to the census in 1872 more than three fifths of the inhabitants of Bombay are orthodox Hindus under Brahminical domination; 140,000—more than one fourth the whole number—are Mussulmans, and only 15,000—scarcely one forty-fifth—are Buddhists. A few thousand Jews, Chinese, Africans, and a mixture of all nationalities make up the total. Accordingly you may imagine the heterogeneous character of the throng in the streets of Bombay, and guess what an infinite variety of types, forms, customs, and manners are here mingled together. Perhaps in no other city on the globe are more languages heard than in Bombay—especially in the European quarter, where every known tongue has its representative. One of the most important components of the population of Bombay—as well as in all Indian cities—is the Parsee, or Guebre. They number about 50,000—only one twelfth of the whole number—but their enterprise and industry have won for them such influence that they play a prominent part in all the affairs of the city. They are descended from those ancient Persians who, after the conquest of Persia by the Mohammedans in the seventh century, refused to accept the faith of their conquerors, and clung tenaciously to the doctrines of Zoroaster. After their expulsion from Persia the Parsees fled to the island of Ormuz, from whence they scattered over India. They marry only among themselves, consequently the purity of their race is preserved. Aside from their peculiar dress, they may, at a first glance, easily be distinguished from all the other races. The men are tall and stately—most of them corpulent; they have yellowish complexions, and are on the whole a handsomer and more robust people than the effeminate Hindus. They wear a peculiar long white cotton gown, wide trousers of the same material, and a tall mitre-shaped hat. Their features express energy and sagacity; they are frugal and sober, and, like the Jews in Europe, thoroughly understand how to accumulate large fortunes. Many of the wealthiest residents of Bombay are Parsees. As hotel-keeper, ship-builder, mechanic, and technicist, the Parsee has won for himself an enviable reputation. They are justly celebrated for their domestic virtues. The dress of the Parsee farmer consists of a single long simply-fashioned garment of some bright color: green, red, yellow, etc. The wealthier Parsee children are frequently seen driving about the streets clad in the most gorgeous raiment of gold and silver embroidered stuffs. Many of them live in beautiful villas, surrounded by all the luxuries, and no doubt arouse the jealous envy of many an impecunious Christian from Europe.

A number of Parsees have founded useful and beneficial institutions; several have been knighted for services rendered the British Government. The public spirit and enterprise of the Parsee, evidences his freedom from priestly domination. His faith—the doctrine of Zoroaster—which is one of the noblest natural religions, is founded on a belief in creative and sustaining powers. Chief among these are the sun and his likeness fire. Multitudes of these sun, or fire-worshippers may be seen on the seashore at sunrise and sunset, devoutly attesting their reverence for the approaching or departing god of day. I confess I never looked with more sympathetic reverence on the devotions of any people than upon these pious sun-worshippers.

Are not we naturalists, who believe that the light and heat of the sun are the primary source of all organic life on our earth, really sun-worshippers?

The religious practices of the Parsees are extremely simple, and, like those of the Mussulmans, based chiefly on judicious sanitary laws, as, for instance, strict dieatry regulations and daily ablutions.

In consequence of these rigid observances the Parsee enjoys perfect health, and his active healthy children impress one more favorably than do the pale-faced, languid offspring of the European resident.

One of the most remarkable customs of the Parsees is their method of disposing of the dead. On the rocky crest of Malabar Hill, from whence the admiring beholder looks down on a magnificent panorama of city, sea, and bay, the Parsees own a beautiful plot of ground which is ornamented with lofty palms and flowering plants. In this garden or cemetery stands the Dakhma, or "Tower of Silence." The interior of this structure is divided into three circular or concentric chambers, each of which is in turn divided into numerous smaller chambers. The inner circle is for the bodies of children, the next for the women, and the outer circle for the men. When a corpse is brought to the cemetery by the relatives it is received by attendants clad in white robes, and, amid the chanting of priests is placed in one of the compartments of the Dakhma. Almost immediately the "holy birds of Ormuzd," the sedate vultures perched on the Palmyra palms in the cemetery, swoop down into the open tower, and in a few minutes devour the flesh of the dead body. Swarms of ravens follow and voraciously swallow the remnants of this feast. Later the bleached bones are gathered into a receptacle under the tower. To most Europeans this is a horrible mode of sepulture; but, as collating zoologist, I confess I think the swift destruction of a dead body by vigorous birds of prey, or by fire, as with the Hindus, more æsthetic and poetical than the slow, wasting, worm-eating corruption of the grave— a method that is just as revolting as that of the Parsees. Besides it is in opposition to all sanitary laws, and is often the source of dangerous disease.

Among the pleasantest excursions I made while in Bombay was one to the palm-groves of Mahim, in company with my host Herr Blaschek. It was a delightful Sunday morning—my first in India—and I shall never forget its many charming impressions. To fully enjoy the perfect freshness of a morning in the tropics one must rise before the sun; accordingly the first sunbeams of this cloudless and beautiful Sunday found us already riding among the gigantic old banyans at the northern foot of Cumbala Hill.

The native huts in the shelter of these large trees, frequently entirely hidden among the root-branches, were the theatre of those original domestic scenes which so divert the European stranger. Whole families in the costume of the Garden of Eden squatted along the roadside, and gave additional lustre to their brown skins by copious applications of cocoa-oil. At the same time affectionate brothers and sisters, or perhaps parents and children, were engaged in a vigorous search for the tiny, slowly-creeping insect that populates the long black hair of their heads, but being devout Hindus, and not permitted to take life, however insignificant, the little captives were merely set to one side; some of the natives were resorting to more efficacious remedies—shaving their heads, or bathing in the pools by the wayside. Others were indolently stretched under the trees, or among the branches.

Far more interesting were the sights in the palm-groves of Mahim, where the "toddy-tapper" climbed nimbly to the tops of the tallest palms to collect the sap which had accumulated during the night, or dextrously swung himself from tree to tree on the ropes stretched between them. Other native laborers were busy with the morning meal.

As for me, I never wearied watching the lovely effects of the sunlight among the quivering foliage and graceful stems of the noble cocoas, and on the giant leaves of the bananas at their feet. Flowers also bloomed everywhere, and these, as well as the butterflies and moths hovering over them, were noticeable for their extraordinary size, gorgeous hues, and singular form. Here and there waved clumps of graceful bamboos of which the huts scattered throughout the grove are built and thatched. Along the paths wandered all kinds of domestic animals, pigs and dogs, chickens and ducks; and sporting among them, the charming forms of the naked Hindu children with their great black questioning eyes!

After we had rambled through the grove for an hour or more we set out for the seashore; but the path we chose soon led us to an extensive morass. Fortunately a two-wheeled bullock-cart driven by a Hindu lad came up with us; we climbed into this elegant conveyance, and after nearly sticking fast in the mire once or twice, were safely hauled to solid ground. On the shore we saw groups of the curious pandanus or screw-pines, whose adventitious roots made them appear as if standing on stilts. The spiral stem forks at the top like a candelabra, every branch bearing a foliated tuft. Immense cobwebs from one to two metres across were stretched between the branches. These were the property of beautifully marked spiders of enormous size, their bodies alone measuring six centimetres, and their slender legs ten centimetres. To capture one of the little monsters was not a very difficult task, and he soon found his death in my spirit bottle. The threads of his web were astonishingly firm and tenacious, as strong almost as linen twine. While we were engaged in the exciting spider-chase a flock of green parrots—the first I had seen in their native freedom—flew screaming from the tops of the palms.

A succession of zoological surprises awaited me on the sands, which the ebb-tide had left exposed for quite a distance. Here I found lovely specimens of the blue medusa (*Crambessa*) which measured more than a foot in diameter, and a globe-fish (*Diodon*) with a prickly hide and inflated abdomen. In the sand were numbers of mussels and snails—all of them characteristic of Indian waters—which I had seen only in the zoological collections of different European museums. I also found some serpulidans, a variety of crustaceans (among them the nimble sand-crab), and numerous fish skeletons, mingled with the skulls and other parts of the human anatomy. The latter were the remains of the low-caste Hindus who had been buried in the sand on the shore. These and other zoological treasures filled my specimen case to overflowing when, at noon, we set out on our return to the city.

Another very interesting part of Bombay is the sacred village of Walkeschwan, which is but a short distance from the bungalow of my host—between it and the governor's house on Malabar Point. I frequently, and at different periods of the day, visited this singular precinct, which is inhabited only by Hindus of the highest caste, and on every visit found something to excite my astonishment and wonder. No member of a lower caste is allowed to defile this sacred spot by his unclean presence. The centre of attraction in Walkeschwan, as in all other sacred communities, is the square pool or tank of water which is reached by broad flights of steps. It is enclosed on all sides by numerous temples and kiosks. The former are ornamented with the characteristic white domes—some of which are shaped like a mitre, others like a broad, low obelisk.

The temples, like the huts of the natives, open toward the street; in the middle of the single pillared hall lies a sacred bull adorned with flowers. Other objects of adoration—singular stone symbols of the Phallic worship—are placed at various points throughout the village and its suburbs. These are smeared with red paint, and are devoutly worshipped by childless people who paste bits of gilt paper on them, and by offerings of flowers hope to be blessed with offspring. On the steps of the temples, or on those leading to the sacred pool, crouch the holy penitents engaged in most peculiar devotional exercises. Most of these fakirs are impostors who enjoy their *dolce far niente* at the expense of a credulous and benevolent community. Their naked bodies are smeared with oil and ashes, and their long hair, which is never combed, represents a peculiar kind of *plica Polonica*—a densely-populated zoological territory!

One merit these fanatics may justly claim: strength to endure persistent self-torture. One old fellow has kept his fist clenched until the finger-nails have grown through the palm of his hand. Another has held his arm in an upright position until it has lost all feeling and power of motion. A third has gashed his face and body, and by constantly applying ashes to the wounds, has kept them in a state of suppuration until he is a revolting sight to behold. It is a well-known fact that religious delusions will lead a man into all sorts of madness and folly—especially if he be under the domination of priestly impostors—but few religions require the extreme measures of the Brahma cultus.

My frequent sketching tours through the sacred village enabled me to study the habits of the privileged class of idlers frequenting the temples. The principal occupation of these noble Brahmans who, as *bona-fide* mendicant friars, subsist on the charity of the superstitious and generous Hindus of the lower castes, seems to be a luxurious inaction and forbearance from labor. Only on rare occasions is their philosophical indolence interrupted by external religious exercises—among which the ablutionary performances at least are to be commended. On such occasions the pool is filled with bathers of both sexes. I was greatly amused by the merry, clothing-disdaining youths that crowded around me to comment on the sketches I had made of the bathers. They were especially diverted by the caricature I had executed of a howling, wildly-gesticulating fakir. These lads were evidently not yet infected with the orthodoxy of their parents. The school in Walkeschwan also furnished some interesting subjects for my sketch-book. The old gray-haired teacher was immensely gratified to learn that I was a colleague of his—a piece of information I conveyed to him through pantomime.

In the immediate vicinity of the temple of wisdom I had

an opportunity to learn something about the Hindu science of physics. A difficult *accouchement* was performed, with the most remarkable instruments, in the public thoroughfare, while a constable or policeman maintained order among the assembled lookers-on, and graciously explained to me the importance of the affair! Near by a second Hindu Esculapius by a series of punches and thumps was exorcising the devil from the pain-racked form of a rheumatic patient.

The celebrated cave-temples on the island of Elephanta were also visited; but, as they have already been described and illustrated in the numerous books of Indian travel, I shall confine my observations to a brief confession of disappointment. They did not come up with my expectations; I had imagined them far more magnificent and imposing. Actual beauty is out of the question in the grotesque sculptures and superfluous ornamentation of the Indian temples. The disgusting and unnatural combinations of human and animal forms, the deities with three heads, distorted features, eight arms and legs, etc., are extremely repugnant to me. I am one of the few heretics who share Goethe's opinions of the "distorted and crazy temples of Elephanta." However, the temples of Elephanta, with their sculptured minutiæ, remarkable pillared halls and emblems, cut from the living rock, will amply repay the curious visitor. We made the excursion from Bombay in a small steam launch, from which we had a superb view of the harbor and mountains and of the Concan coast, between which and Bombay lie the island of Elephanta, and the bare red rocks of Trombay Island. I shall always remember Elephanta, for it was there I first looked on the wonderful exuberance of the tropical flora in its natural state. Of course I had visited the Victoria Botanic Garden, which contains a number of the most beautiful of tropical plants, such as palms, bamboos, bananas, pandanus, breadfruit, papaya, lotus, pistachio, etc.; but the pleasure I experienced in the Garden is not to be compared with my delight when I beheld, on Elephanta, India's most imposing flora growing with the wanton luxuriance which is intolerant of garden restraint. Here lianas of all sorts, and climbing ferns clothe the trunks of giant teaks; here the noblest cocoa-palms incline their graceful stems toward the shore which is fringed with curious pandanus shrubs, and fortified to the very water's edge by a wall of mangrove roots. Here the parasitic fig, convolvuli, and other creepers twine around the black upright stems of the mighty Palmyra palms. Here are magnificent banyans, from whose wide-spreading branches depend huge air-roots, which in time take root in the ground, and become supports to the mother crown. And there—see! there is a powerful murderer (a parasitic vine) strangling a noble palm in his deadly embrace, and a little farther on the fellow's brother clasps the dead trunk of his victim in his leafless and withered arms—the tree died first, then the same fate overtook his murderer.

Among all these the slender bamboo holds aloft his huge bouquet; bananas and plantains expand their broad green plumes; deliciously-fragrant blossoms unfold their chalices; the feathery acacia unfolds its delicate canopy; prickly euphorbias interweave their stems into dense hedges. Thus, on Elephanta, the tropical vegetation of which I had read and dreamed for thirty years became at last a palpable reality.

Among all these vegetable beauties thousands of gorgeous insects hung in the sun-warmed air; huge brilliant buprestidans hummed through the thickets; hundreds of agile lizards and snakes darted among the undergrowth; flocks of gay-plumaged birds flew screaming harshly from branch to branch—all new, never before seen alive or out of a museum!

And yet they were all old acquaintances. Like a happy child I darted after the enchanting creatures, laid hold of the trees and plants to convince myself that I was not dreaming of fairy-land.

My brief stay in Bombay admitted of but one extended tour to the mainland—an excursion to Lanaulie and the Karli cave-temples. In company with a fellow-traveler on the *Helios*—Count Hunyady—I left Bombay at noon on the 11th of November. Delightful weather favored us; at times, however, the sun became a trifle too ardent—the mercury registering in the shade at noon 30° R. The nights were proportionately warm, the thermometer once at midnight marking 25°. The railway journey to Lanaulie is one of five hours' duration, and ours drew from us, besides copious perspiration, many a sigh over the torrid atmosphere. And yet the first-class coach in which we traveled had all the modern appliances for comfort: the double roof projected on either side; there were blinds and green glass for the windows; cool leather-cushioned seats; ingenious devices for ventilation, and best of all, small compartments in which one might refresh one's self with a bath in cool water. Each of the first-class coaches contains two saloons which accommodate but six passengers. The seats or sofas —of which there are three, two lengthwise and one across— are transformed into comfortable beds at night; three additional beds are put up four feet above the lower ones, thus forming six couches which are larger and much more comfortable than the berths in the cabin of a ship.

The traveler's portmanteau is disposed of by the porter; he may promenade at will through the little saloon and enjoy a view of the fleeting landscape from the numerous windows. The prospect was of exceeding interest to me, and I was happily able to secure a number of satisfactory sketches of the country we traversed during the five hours' ride. The railway which traverses a large section of Bombay, passes Byculla, Parell, and Sassoon, then crosses a bridge over the narrow arm of the sea between Bombay and Salsette Islands, then another bridge to the mainland of Hither India. Our route for several hours was over the flat lowland of Concan; numerous villages of wretched bamboo huts and several larger but unimportant towns gave us an idea of the Mahratta population of this region.

During the rainy season (from June to September) the extensive plains of the coast are covered with a luxuriant growth of tall grass, and, in some places, are cultivated with rice, corn, etc. When we crossed them the vegetation was withered, and the broad grassy stretches sere and yellow. The evergreen plants alone retained their fresh tint, the banana and fig trees, and that important treasure of the Concan flora, the stately Palmyra palm (*Borassus flabelliformis*). Thousands or rather millions of this noble tree are everywhere visible— now in groups, now alone— giving the lowland its characteristic physiognomy. Like the cocoa and date-palms, the Palmyra palm is one of the most useful plants—almost every part of it is used for one or more domestic or technical purposes. Especially attractive were the groves of this tree on the banks of the reed-fringed ponds past which we steamed. These miniature lakes, together with the naked brown forms of the natives, the two-wheeled bullock-carts, the wallowing buffaloes, and the little square reed huts, formed a lovely picture, beyond which towered the jagged crest of the Bhor-Ghaut.

At Kurjut, at the foot of the mountain, the light locomotive which had brought us from Bombay was exchanged for one adapted to the heavier grade (1.37) before us, and soon the ascent became clearly perceptible—rising over 2000 feet in a few hours. Numerous turrets and viaducts, as well as the sudden turns of the road, remind one of the picturesque roads in the Alps—the Semmering and the Brenner. (The steepest grade on the latter is only 1.40.)

The landscape assumes an entirely different character; the palms which abundantly adorn the lowland country disappear, and in their room appear mighty, umbrageous forest trees, the stately tobacco plant, and the wool-tree with its immense leaves.

The escarpment of the tabular highland, which in some places presents a succession of steps or terraces, is here and there cloven by deep gorges; these are clothed with dense masses of shrubbery which give the mountain a European character, although the peculiar configuration of the Bhor-Ghaut is very little like any range in Europe. Now these stupendous rock-masses rise to a perpendicular wall of more than a thousand feet; now they present a succession of broad, truncated pyramids; now a mural front whose battlements and turrets at a distance appear like a mighty fortress. Although the plutonic masses which form the Bhor-Ghaut (they are principally black trap and basaltic syenite) are totally different from the stratified sandstone of our Swiss mountains, yet, in its exterior configuration, this isolated table-land in some places is strikingly similar to them.

As sudden as the transformation in the landscape, from a scene of tropical splendor in the 19th degree of latitude to one of more austere character in the 53d degree, is the change of the air we breathe. A breezy coolness succeeds the oppressive heat of the lowlands, and it is with unspeakable delight that we inhale the invigorating mountain air. One only fully appreciates the benefits of a temperate climate when under the enervating influence of the tropical sun.

The higher we ascend the more like home it seems; but this allusion is rudely dispelled by the information that, two years ago, in the ravine below us, an English officer was killed by a tiger. Two streams of water here fall from a considerable height, and in the rainy season form copious waterfalls; but at present they are mere threads of moisture, and sparse yellow grass covers the spaces which are not overgrown with jungle.

Shortly before reaching Lanaulie we passed Matheron Station, which is a favorite summer resort for the wealthier residents of Bombay. Beautiful views of the surrounding country may be had from various elevations in the neighborhood. A singular rock formation near Matheron is called the "Duke's Nose"—in honor, I believe, of the Duke of Wellington!

It was quite dark when at seven o'clock we arrived at Lanaulie—2100 feet above the sea—and found really tolerable quarters in the diminutive "hotel" kept by a Parsee. Before retiring for the night we made arrangements for an excursion the next morning to the Karli caves, Buddhist rock-temples which, in extent and wealth of sculptures, surpass all others of a like character in India. We engaged ponies for a five-o'clock start; but when we made our appearance at the appointed hour we found that a stately coach, drawn by two horses, had been substituted by the cunning landlord for the little mountain ponies we had hired. Although dissatisfied with this arrangement, which was a more profitable one for the landlord, we took our places in the coach, which conveyed us about half a mile over a good road; then we were obliged to continue the journey on foot for more than a mile through fields and meadows, and at last up an almost precipitous hill.

The caves are situated half way up the western declivity of a trachyte hill that rises more than a thousand feet above the plateau of Lanaulie. The Karli cave-temples are much older and larger than the Brahman cave-temples of Elephanta; the sculptures are less complex and grotesque; the representations of human and animal forms more natural; they are, on the whole, the most perfect structures of the kind in existence.

Like the temples of Elephanta, and many others of a similar character in India, those of Karli, as well as the forms of man and beast profusely ornamenting the walls, are excavated and cut from the solid rock. The lofty interior of the Tschaitya temple, a gigantic vault resembling the interior of a hollow cylinder, is divided by two rows of columns, with a broad central nave and two narrow side aisles. The numerous male and female statues, elephants, lions, etc., as well as the pillars and door-posts, are very ingeniously carved from the hard black trap-rock, and smoothly polished. Above, and on either side of this temple, are a number of smaller excavations, from which, at our approach, flew swarms of bats. Several priests who pass their lives in these solitudes solicited alms from us, and while they mumbled prayers of gratitude for the gifts bestowed, harsh cries sounded from the rocks above us. On looking up we beheld a number of large black apes, which were the first I had seen in their untamed state, and which, on comparison with the dirty, naked, begging monks, seemed quite respectable as ancestors.

III.

COLOMBO.

ON the 21st of November, amid the glorious effulgence of a cloudless tropical morning, I set foot on that ever-verdant wonder-island on which I was to spend four of the most enjoyable and edifying months of my life. The *Helios*, which had brought us in five days of uninterruptedly fair weather over a sea as smooth as glass, from Bombay to Ceylon, sighted the island at midnight on the 20th, and the first gray dawn was just breaking when I went on deck to behold, as soon as possible, the "promised land" of my scientific longings.

Before us in the east, above the dim mirror of the Indian Ocean, lay a slender, misty bank that, when the brief morning twilight of the tropics gave place to the swiftly approaching day, revealed itself as the cocoa-fringed west coast of Ceylon. The conical peak towering conspicuously above the mountain chain of the central highlands was

Adam's Peak—world-famed for the superstitious myths and legends which envelop it. When the brilliant sun appeared above the mountains we were able to distinguish a second and lower range of hills between the highlands of the interior and the coast. Soon the snowy-stemmed cocoa-palms became clearly discernible, and on approaching nearer, the salient features of Ceylon's chief city, Colombo, also stood revealed.

Directly in front of us lay the fort and the harbor, on the right (to the south) the suburb of Colpetty, on the left (north) the pettah, or "Black Town."

To me the cloudless sky and fresh, aromatic breeze which favored my first view of the long-dreamed-of island were signs of good luck. Usually in the morning the mountains are either wholly or partially obscured by heavy mists. The first boat to approach our vessel was that of the pilot who took us into the harbor, where we were soon surrounded by boats of a shape peculiar to the South Asiatic islands. These are hollow logs of perhaps twenty feet in length, three feet in depth and scarcely one and a half feet in width—so narrow that a grown person cannot sit in them without placing one foot behind the other. At the extremity of two elastic outriggers, which extend from one side of the boat, is a balance-log that gives an astonishing degree of security to the frail craft. As I had occasion later to use these singular canoes for my zoological excursions, I had an opportunity to test their advantages as well as to experience their disadvantages. At first sight of their picturesque form, however, only my artistic perceptions were aroused; perhaps too I was influenced by their Singhalese crews—in their way quite as rare and peculiar as the boats themselves.

The natives crowded the decks of the *Helios* and offered for sale fruits, fish, and other products of their country, as well as trifling articles of their industry. Most of them wore only the "comboy" or "sarong," a piece of red cotton cloth that hung, apron-fashion, from a belt at the waist. They wear their long black hair in a knot fastened at the back of the head with a tortoise-shell comb, a style of coiffure that increases the effeminate appearance of their slender figures, small feet and hands, and delicate features. The nude black Tamils, whose coal-boats surrounded the

Helios, are a sturdier race of people than the Singhalese; there is also a marked difference between these two races and the moormen, stately fellows in long white caftans, trunk-hose, and yellow turbans, who deal in precious stones, shells, and silver ornaments. The prices demanded for these articles are usually three or four, sometimes ten times their actual value; one of our passengers paid one rupee for a brilliant stone that had been offered but a few moments before for eighty rupees! This "precious stone," like most of the "gems" of the "Ruby Island," was nothing but the product of some ingenious European manufacturer of ground glass. Gems of this sort are imported from Europe in large quantities every year.

My reception from Herr Stipperger, the agent of the Austrian Lloyd in Colombo, to whom I had letters of introduction from that company, as well as from mutual friends in Triest and Bombay, was most cordial. Without further ceremony he invited me to become his guest while I remained in Colombo, and did everything in his power to render my stay both pleasant and profitable. If, during my four months' sojourn in Ceylon I saw and enjoyed, learned and accomplished, more than many other travelers could have done in a whole year, then I owe it all to the generous kindness of my "Singhalese Providenza," as I jestingly dubbed my friend Stipperger. This gentleman, who is a native of Vienna, and only a few years my senior, was formerly in the Austrian navy, from which he entered the service of the Austrian Lloyd Company. I can only wish that his present position may amply recompense his manifold and distinguished abilities. After cordially bidding adieu to the officers and passengers on the *Helios*, who were going to Singapore and Hong Kong, I quitted the gallant ship which had brought me so safely and pleasantly from Triest, and accompanied Herr Stipperger in a boat to the land. Through the kind intervention of the latter gentleman, and with the aid of the official documents from the government in England to the governor of Ceylon, my numerous luggage passed toll-free through the customs, and was spared the usual official examination—a formidable task indeed with my sixteen trunks and boxes!

From the quay we drove to the office of the Austrian Lloyd, and from there to breakfast in a club-house. Then

I devoted the first hours after my arrival to making several necessary visits, and delivered the several important letters of introduction which the German consul at Colombo, Herr Freudenberg (at present in Germany) had been kind enough to give me.

In this manner I spent the morning and part of the afternoon of my first day in Ceylon. By five o'clock I was ready to accompany Herr Stipperger in his light two-wheeled calash, drawn by a fleet Australian stallion, to his residence "Whist Bungalow," which is a considerable distance (three English miles) from the business centre, or "fort," of the city. Colombo, like Bombay and most of the more important East Indian towns, consists of a European business quarter in the "fort," and several suburbs which contain the habitations of the native population.

The fort at Colombo was built in 1517 by the Portuguese, who were the first European sovereigns on the island. They landed in 1505 and remained perhaps 150 years—about as long as their Dutch successors who drove them from the island. Under the rule of the Dutch, as well as under the English, who took possession of Ceylon in 1796. Colombo maintained its importance as chief city, notwithstanding many other places, especially Point de Galle, were in many respects better calculated for the first place. In late years the British Government has strenuously sought to establish Colombo's precedence as a first-class seaport; consequently it will doubtless continue to occupy its prominent position, all its unfavorable conditions to the contrary notwithstanding.

One would naturally suppose that the chief requirement of a first-class seaport would be a good harbor. This Colombo has not got, while Point de Galle has all the advantages of an extensive and natural roadstead. True, nowadays harbors may be constructed anywhere along a coast by dredging, and by the erection of substantial piers, or breakwaters, as at Port Said, all that is necessary thereto being money.

The English Government constructed a breakwater at the southern extremity of the Colombo harbor, but strong doubts are entertained as to whether this piece of masonry will answer the purpose for which it was built without frequent repairs at an enormous outlay of money and labor.

On the other hand, the natural harbor of Point de Galle might be improved at a much less expense; the few rocks and coral reefs which hinder the passage of large ships might, by the use of dynamite, be easily removed. The contest for supremacy between these two seaports on the west coast of Ceylon, has resulted in the victory of the ancient capital over her rival, although the latter, by virtue of her climate, situation, and environs, is more deserving of the prize. The climate of Colombo is excessively hot and enervating—it is one of the hottest in the world!—while the charming, verdure-clad hills around Point de Galle render it an agreeable and healthful place of residence.

The country around Colombo is flat, and chiefly covered by swamps and stagnant pools. The fort stands on a low headland, of inconsiderable extent, that serves as a landmark of the level west coast of the island. Mention is made of this headland in Ptolemy's ancient geography, on whose excellent map of Ceylon—"Salike"—it is called Jupiter's Cape, *Jovis Extremum*.

The walls of the fort, which were strongly fortified by the Dutch, are still surmounted by cannon, and almost surrounded by water; two thirds of their circumference are washed by the sea, and the remaining third (the south-east side) by the waters of a broad lagoon. Several bridges cross the latter and connect the fort with the mainland. The few short and narrow streets, which cross each other at right angles, are occupied principally by the offices and warehouses of the European merchants, a number of public and government buildings. Among the latter is the "Queen's House," the handsome palace of the governor, which, standing in the midst of the most exuberant tropical vegetation, with roomy pillared halls, large airy saloons, and stately staircase, is the most imposing of the public buildings.

I paid a visit to this stately palace the day after my arrival, and delivered the letters from the English Government to the governor. The interior arrangements are very tasteful and in keeping with the splendor of the British autocrat who rules the island. Numbers of Indian servants in showy livery perform the domestic service of the Queen's House, while red and gold uniformed English soldiers stand guard. Chatham Street, in which the office of the Austrian

Lloyd Company is located, is, like many other streets in Colombo and Point de Galle, embellished with rows of hibiscus trees, whose large crimson or yellow flowers cover the ground in countless numbers. The shops in which I was most interested are also in the same street, bazaars in which you may purchase photographic views of scenery and living animals. The very first hour in Ceylon I had the pleasure of examining some views of the loveliest points in the savage mountain region and along the picturesque coast, as well as a sight of the astonishing wonders of vegetation: palms, pandanus, lianas, tree-ferns, banyans, etc. No less interesting was it for me in that first hour on the wonder-island to make the acquaintance of some of its most attractive fauna, such as apes, axis, or spotted deer, parrots, doves, etc.

On the south side of the fort are the quarters of the English soldiery, large airy barracks which extend to the banks of the lagoon. Adjoining these is the military hospital, and beyond it the esplanade, called here the "Galle-face," because the high road to Point de Galle begins at this point. Afternoons, between the hours of five and six, the esplanade becomes a favorite place of assembly for the wealth and fashion of Colombo.

Here, as in Hyde Park, London, fair ladies and gallant gentlemen meet to recruit from the enervating heat of midday, and to enjoy the sunsets which are always embellished by the most marvellous cloud-pictures. The distinguished young gentlemen of Colombo are mounted on horseback (some of the horses are sorry-looking hacks); while the fair ladies, with bouquets of flowers, and in elegant tropical toilettes, recline gracefully in their comfortable carriages.

As soon as the sun has disappeared everybody hurries home—partly in dread of the fever-laden evening air, and partly because important preparations are to be made for the principal event of the day—dinner, a meal that is here attended with as much ceremony as in "Old England." My first visit to the esplanade was during the hot hour of noon, when I had an opportunity to test the full power of the torrid rays which Helios sheds on such unsheltered tracts. The outlines of objects around me quivered in the heated air, and on the red sand road, between the grass bordering it on either side, I saw a fata morgana—a phenomenon that frequently occurs here. The mirage reflected a sheet of sparkling water that was forded by the wagons and pedestrians coming toward me. The thermometer hanging in the cool rooms of the club-house registered 24 R. Outside in the sun it would probably have risen to 36° or 40°.

Adjoining the esplanade is the suburb of Kolupitya, or Colpetty, which extends towards the south, between the flat, sandy shore and the road, to Galle. On both sides of the road are numbers of elegant villas surrounded by flourishing gardens. This villa-quarter extends in a westerly direction to the so called "Cinnamon Gardens"—a locality that, since the English Government was forced to abandon its cinnamon monopoly, has lost its original importance, and has become the private property of wealthy merchants. "Cinnamon Gardens," with the handsome and costly residences scattered among the trees, is now considered the most aristocratic villa-quarter in Colombo. But its distance from the seashore and the refreshing sea-breeze, as well as its low situation and proximity to the arm of the lagoon, are great disadvantages. The sultry heat here attains its highest altitude, swarms of mosquitoes render the evenings extremely unpleasant, while innumerable frogs of all sorts disturb one's rest by their loud nightly concerts. The same may be said of the adjacent "Slave Island," so called because the Dutch—in the preceding century—at night penned the government slaves here.

And yet, notwithstanding all these disadvantages, this is the most beautiful part of Colombo. The coves denting the shores of the lagoon are encircled by cultivated gardens, above which slender cocoa-palms incline their feathered crests; elegant European villas and picturesque native huts adorn the banks, while a noble background is formed by the distant mountains of the central highlands, above which towers the proud head of the ever-conspicuous Adam's Peak.

An evening canoe ride on the peaceful bosom of the lagoon is one of Colombo's greatest pleasures. North of the above-mentioned suburbs stretches the densely-populated *pettah*, or "Black Town." It extends for more than a mile along the ocean front to the mouth of the Kalany-ganga, from which stream the city took its original name of Kalan-totta, or Kalan-bua.

Ibn Batula in 1340 called it Kalambu, and described it as the "largest and finest city of Serendib"—the ancient Arabian name of the island. Kalambu, under the Portuguese, became Colombo.

Near the wide delta of the stately Kalany, not far from the shore of the Indian Ocean, stands the house of my friend Stipperger, with whom I spent my first pleasant weeks in Ceylon. This section of Colombo, which bears the rather singular name of Mutwal, or Modera, is, to my thinking, one of the most interesting in the whole region. I shall never forget the strange medley which, like the shifting scenes of a *laterna magica*, passed before my astonished gaze as I drove from the fort to Whist Bungalow. In the open huts, under the shadow of the omnipresent cocoa-palm—everywhere in the narrow streets of the *pettah*, one might see how this heterogeneous population lived, moved, and had its being. Here, as in all localities of the Torrid Zone, the domestic economy of the natives is characterized by little or no privacy, for as the heat of the tropical sun renders covering for the human form unnecessary, so, too, the interiors of the huts and bazaars are exposed to the public gaze—neither windows nor doors preventing the outsider from seeing everything that transpires within.

Instead of doors and windows there is a single large opening in the front of the hut or bazaar, that at night, or during inclement weather is closed by a curtain of matting, or a sliding wooden lattice. The artisan may be seen at work in his shop, sometimes in the public thoroughfare, while the most intimate scenes of domestic and family life are not withdrawn from the curious gaze of the public. The peculiar charm of these Indian homes lies partly in this *naïve* publicity of domestic affairs, partly in the primitive simplicity of their requirements—the few household articles attesting this fact—and partly in their harmony with surrounding nature. The little gardens which encircle every hut are so unartificial in their arrangement, the few useful plants which represent the natives' principal possession are grouped so picturesquely around the tiny dwellings, that everything seems to have sprung spontaneously from the fruitful soil. The most important of these useful plants is the "prince of the vegetable kingdom"— the palm—the cocoa-palm in particular. Every part of this tree, which frequently constitutes the sole wealth of the Singhalese, is used for some purpose; accordingly it is seen growing everywhere, in the cities and villages as well as in remote districts. It is the tree which first attracts the eye of the new-comer, and gives character to the landscape. The number of cocoa-palms on the island is about forty millions, and each tree yields from eighty to one hundred nuts (8–10 quarts of oil). The cocoa-palm is not found in the northern half of the island, nor in some parts of the east coast. In these regions its place is supplied by the not less useful Palmyra palm—the same species that covers the arid regions of Hither India, and that grows in such profusion near Bombay. Even at a distance these two palms are very dissimilar. The Palmyra belongs to the fan-palm family, and has a vigorous, perfectly upright black stem that is crowned by a thick tuft of stiff, fan-shaped leaves. The cocoa is a feather-palm; its slender white stem, from sixty to eighty feet high, is gracefully curved, and adorned with a ponderous crown of immense pinnate leaves. The foliage of the elegant Areca palm (*Areca catechu*) is similar, but smaller and less flexible; it has a thin, reed-like, upright stem, is always to be found near the huts of the Singhalese, and bears the favorite nut which, when chewed with the leaves of the betel-pepper, stains the teeth and saliva a red color. Another palm, the kitool (*Caryota urens*), is cultivated chiefly for its abundant saccharine sap, from which are prepared palm-sugar (jaggery) and palm-wine (toddy). Its powerful and vigorous stem supports a crown of double feathery leaves which resemble those of the maidenhair fern (*Adiantum capillus veneris*). The bread-fruit and mango trees in the little gardens, rank next in importance to the palms. Of the former there are two kinds: the true bread-fruit (*Artocarpus incisa*) and the jack-tree (*Artocarpus integrifolia*), magnificent specimens of which are to be found everywhere, and among them frequently the singular cotton tree (*Bombax*). Mingled with these may also be found the beautiful banana or pisang plant, which certainly deserves its name of "fig of Paradise." Its golden fruit, eaten raw or cooked, is very nutritious and wholesome. Its huge pale-green plumes drooping from a stem twenty or thirty feet high are the loveliest decorations of the Singhalese huts. Scarcely less effective for ornamental purposes is the barbed foliage of the Caladium—which is cultivated for its esculent root—and the palmate leaves of the pretty manihot shrub—a member of the Euphorbiaceæ family. The exquisite green of these plants contrasts finely with the brown clay huts and the warm red tint of the soil (the result probably of an excess of oxide of iron). In perfect accord with these tints is the cinnamon hue of the Singhalese complexion, and the deep black skins of the Tamils. In Colombo, as well as on the south and west coasts of Ceylon, the Singhalese constitute the majority of the population. The name Singhalese is given to the descendants of the Indian Hindus who, according to the Pali chronicle, the *Mahawanso*, in the year 543 B.C., under Wijayo, invaded Ceylon and subdued the aboriginal inhabitants of the island. Of the latter race, the Veddahs—a tribe of outcasts inhabiting the interior—are believed to be the descendants.

The Singhalese were in turn driven from the northern half of the island, as well as from the east coast and a large portion of the central highlands, by the Malabars, or Tamils, who came from Southern Hindustan, from the Malabar coast. In stature, physiognomy, complexion, language, religion, and customs, the Tamils are very different from the Singhalese. They belong to another branch of the Aryan genealogical tree. The Singhalese dialect seems to have sprung from the Pali language, while the Malabars speak the entirely dissimilar Tamil language. The religion of the former is Buddhism; that of the latter Hinduism, or Brahmanism. The Singhalese are devoted principally to agriculture, the cultivation of palms, bananas, and other useful plants; but are, nevertheless, very shy of hard work. This is usually accomplished by the Malabars, who, in the lowlands, work on the roads, are builders, carriers, coachmen, etc., and in the highlands find employment on the coffee plantations. At the present time the Malabars (large numbers of whom yearly immigrate from the Indian peninsula) constitute, perhaps, one third of Ceylon's inhabitants, while the Singhalese number three fifths of the whole population, which is about two and a half millions.

Next to the Singhalese and Malabars the Indo-Arabians or moormen, form—according to number and influence—the most important part of the native population of Ceylon. They number perhaps 150,000, or one tenth the number of Singhalese. They are descended from those Arabs who, more than 2000 years ago, gained a firm foothold in Ceylon, as well as in other parts of Southern and South-eastern Asia, and who, between the eighth and tenth centuries (until the arrival of the Portuguese) conducted the principal commercial interests of the island. The entire retail as well as a great part of the wholesale trade of Ceylon is still in the hands of these active and enterprising sons of the desert, who, by their speculative wisdom, craft, and pre-eminent skill for money-making, here play a similar rôle to that of the Jews in Europe. In many other respects they are like their remote kinsmen in Europe, who have no representatives in Ceylon.

The language spoken and written by the moormen is a mixture of Arabian and Tamil. They are chiefly Mohammedans and Sunnites. Their complexion is a brownish-yellow, their physiognomy unmistakably Semitic. Hair and beard are generally long and black. Their powerful frames, which are clad in long white burnous and wide white trousers, appear all the more stately among the Tamils and Singhalese, because of the tall yellow turbans —shaped like a bishop's mitre—they wear on their heads.

In addition to these three predominant races, the population of Ceylon is made up of aboriginal tribes, the Veddahs and Rodiyas (of whom there are perhaps 2000), Malays and Javanese (who are principally enlisted as soldiers), Parsees and Afghans (mostly money-changers and usurers), Negroes and Caffres (soldiers and servants). The offspring of these different native races by intermarriage with Europeans, exhibit the most diverse characteristics, and offer interesting difficulties to anthropological classification. To these belong the "Burghers," the descendants of the Portuguese and the Dutch, in whose veins runs more or less Singhalese or Tamil blood. This class furnishes the clerks and accountants in the offices and warehouses, the subordinate officers of the government, in which positions they are highly esteemed. Lastly, the number of Europeans—the "foreign" rulers of the island—is only about three or four thousand, and these are chiefly English and Scotch. In the cities they occupy all the higher government offices, and own all the larger commercial houses. In the mountain districts they form the numerous and remarkable class of "planters" with whose peculiar mode of life I became familiar during my travels through the highlands.

According to the census of 1857 (twenty-five years ago), the total number of inhabitants in Ceylon then was only 1,760,000. In 1871 (eleven years ago), it had increased to 2,405,000, and at the present time there are over 2,500,000 souls on the island.

If we assume that the number of inhabitants amounts to the round sum of two and a half millions, then the constituent parts may be divided as follows:

Singhalese (principally Buddhists)	1,500,000
Tamils or Malabars (mostly Hindus)	820,000
Indo-Arabians or moormen (chiefly Mohammedans)	150,000
Mixed	10,000
Malays, Chinese, Caffres, and Negroes	8,000
Burghers (half-breed)	6,000
Europeans (chiefly English)	4,000
Veddahs (aborigines)	2,000
Total	2,500,000

As the superficial area of Ceylon is 1250 geographical square miles, scarcely one sixth less than that of Ireland, it might very easily accommodate six or eight times its present population. According to the ancient chronicles, Ceylon, 2000 years ago, contained many more inhabitants—perhaps more than twice its present number! The depopulated and, to some extent, desolate northern half of the island was in those days densely populated; and where now impassable jungles afford secure retreats for apes and bears, parrots and doves, flourished extensive fields, rendered productive by a system of irrigation that is worthy all admiration. The remains of these irrigation tanks, as well as the noble ruins of the vanished cities, Anarajapoora, Sigiri, Pollanarua, etc, to this day bear witness of their former magnificence. They show what might again be accomplished on this "jewel-island," this "noblest pearl in the diadem of India."

IV.

WHIST BUNGALOW.

THIS charming villa stands, as I mentioned before, at the northern extremity of Colombo, or rather Mutwal, near where the Kalany River debouches on the sea. It is a good hour's distance from the business centre of the city; and its isolated situation in the midst of natural beauties, its distance from the noise and tumult of the fort, as well as from the favorite villa-quarters, Colpetty and Cinnamon Gardens, made it peculiarly attractive in my eyes.

Another weighty reason, perhaps, for my partiality towards Whist Bungalow was the hospitable treatment I received from its several occupants. Besides Herr Stipperger, there were three other very agreeable countrymen of mine.

The "few days" I at first proposed to remain with Herr Stipperger soon extended to a "few weeks," and as I made another visit of several days to the bungalow on my return from the south, one month of the four passed on the island was pleasantly spent in this delightful spot.

Whist Bungalow owes its peculiar name to the fact that the first proprietor of the secluded villa, an old English officer, at the beginning of the present century, was wont, on Sundays, to invite his comrades to a whist-party. As the rigid observances of the English Church would have condemned these merry card-parties as a profanation of the Sabbath they were kept a profound secret; and the more the assembled warriors rejoiced at being able thus to escape the tedium of the English Sunday and an orthodox society, the more boisterous became the whist-parties—and their consequent drinking-bouts—in the solitary bungalow.

At that time Whist Bungalow was a simple little cottage hidden in the dense shrubbery of the garden. Its present stately proportions were assumed under the proprietorship of a Mr. Morgan, an advocate, who was a gay man of the world, and who expended a large part of his fortune in enlarging and embellishing the villa—a little Miramare of Ceylon—and making it worthy of its romantically beautiful situation. The choicest ornamental trees and shrubs were planted in the garden. A stately colonnade, with airy veranda, encircled the enlarged mansion, while its lofty saloons were furnished with princely magnificence. For many a year Whist Bungalow was the scene of gay parties and feasts which were far more luxurious and costly, if not so boisterous and merry, than the less ostentatious revels of the whist-players. It seems, however, that Mr. Morgan's large income was not sufficient for the colossal expenditures of his Lucullan mode of life; he died unexpectedly, when it was found that a considerable deficit existed in his cash account. The numerous creditors seized Whist Bungalow, and were glad at last to sell it at public auction in order to realize at least a portion of the money they had loaned Mr. Morgan.

And now came a turning-point in the history of the princely mansion, whose new proprietor was not long allowed to rejoice in his bargain. Rumor, who had already whispered many strange tales concerning the romantic bungalow, now asserted audibly that it was "haunted" by the spirit of the suddenly deceased Mr. Morgan. Every night—moonlight or not—the ghost was said to appear, attended by hideous noises; white forms meandered through the saloons; winged demons fluttered in the pillared halls; and equally unearthly creatures with flaming eyes perambulated the roof. The director-general of this ghostly crew was, of course, the spirit of Mr. Morgan, of whom it was now said that his suddenly evaporated wealth had not been obtained by strictly honorable means; that he, like some others of his calling, had employed his extensive legal knowledge less in the interest of his clients than to find means for transferring the contents of their treasure-chests into his own. He was also said to have embezzled large sums; to have defrauded widows and orphans. etc. etc.; for all of which the divagations of his spirit among the scenes of his former Bacchanalia was the punishment.

So many natives in the near neighborhood of Mutwal had heard the ghostly clatter—some had even seen the terrible demons—that the new proprietor of Whist Bungalow would not live in it himself, nor could he find a tenant for it.

Thus Whist Bungalow stood deserted and empty when my friend Stipperger heard of it, and, on seeing the charming place, decided to rent it. But this had also its difficulties. No servant willing to live in the haunted house was to be found. This was accomplished only after substantial proofs of the ghost's zoological origin had been established. The first night Herr Stipperger spent in his new home he armed himself to the teeth, and awaited the appearance of the spirits, who proved to be, as he had conjectured, corporeal mammals of flesh and blood with whom the defunct Mr. Morgan was not in the least analogous. The mysterious noises, when silenced by a load of shot, proved to be a congress of wild-cats; the ghosts of the saloons and pillared halls manifested themselves as huge bandicoot rats and flying foxes (*Pteropus*). The evidence furnished by this night's chase was so overwhelming that the fears of the most timid servant were vanquished, and my friend took peaceable possession of the isolated Whist Bungalow. Order was at once restored to the large garden which had become a wilderness; the dismantled rooms were furnished anew, and when several German countrymen saw the restored villa they were so charmed with its appearance they begged the new tenant to sublet several of its numerous apartments to them. This was done; and when I arrived at Whist Bungalow I found there the quartette, with whom I passed many a pleasant evening in conversation. There was never any lack of diverse individual opinion, which, with us Germans, is quite indispensable— the famous "German Unity" to the contrary notwithstanding. Herr Both, from Hanau (to whom I am indebted for a neat collection of reptiles), represented the Frankfort district of Germany in Ceylon; Herr Suhren, from East Friesland (who presented me with a collection of beautiful butterflies), the extreme north-west; and Herr Herath, from Bayreuth (who delighted me with gifts of birds of paradise, parrots, and honey-birds), the Bavarian region of the Fatherland.

The peculiar charm of Whist Bungalow over all other Colombo residences, lies partly in its delightful situation, and partly in its magnificent surroundings. While the out-buildings—servants' quarters, stables, etc.—lie hidden behind the garden, the main structure stands on the bank of a lovely stretch of water that extends along the west side of the garden. The airy veranda commands a view of the ocean, of the mouth of the Kalany-ganga, and of a lovely little wooded island in its delta. Farther towards the north the eye follows a belt of cocoa-forest that stretches along the coast to Negombo. On the south, contiguous to the garden of Whist Bungalow, lies a picturesque tract of land over which, with a charming disregard for order, are scattered fishing-huts under slender cocoa-palms, between them a diminutive Buddha temple, and beyond them the rocks of the shore, ornamented with grotesque pandanus shrubs, etc. From this point a narrow sandy tongue of land juts in a northerly direction towards the mouth of the river, and, stretching in front of our garden, forms a peaceful little inland sea. The tongue of land which separates this lake from the adjacent ocean is densely overgrown with the lovely crimson-flowered goat's-foot (*Ipomea pes capri*), and the singular water-pink (*Spinifex squarrosus*). It also serves as *terra firma* for several fishing-huts, and all day long a succession of animated and interesting pictures may be seen along its strand. In the early morning, before the sun has risen, the fishermen and their families here take their morning bath, then the horses and oxen take theirs. Industrious washers are busy from morning till night beating the clothes on smooth stones, or spreading them on the bank to dry. Numerous fishing craft sail up and down, and evenings, when they are drawn on the beach, and their large square sails stretched out to dry, the tongue of land, with the long row of motionless boats, affords an exceedingly picturesque sight—especially if the sails are swelled by the evening breeze, and the setting sun, just dipping into the ocean, floods the entire Indian coast with radiant gold, orange, and purple.

According to information received from my friends, this sandy tongue has frequently changed in form. It is, in fact, one of those movable bars which are found fronting the outlets of all the larger rivers of Ceylon. The latter, in their wild course from the mountains, bring with them masses of gravel and sand, to which, in their more leisurely progress through the low coast-land, the abundant rains add large quantities of earth and mud. All this deposited at the mouths of the rivers in a short time forms considerable bars. The shape, size, and position of these bars is constantly changing, according to the direction taken by the outlets of the river through its level delta. In former times the principal outlet of the Kalany-ganga was a mile farther to the south, through the Cinnamon Gardens. The lagoons in that suburb, which are still connected with the Kalany by narrow canals, are the remnants of the former outlet; the largest portion of Colombo then occupied the delta of the river. In a like manner the picturesque bar opposite Whist Bungalow was at one time connected with the mainland at its northern extremity, at another time by its southern point, while the wooded islet in the principal outlet of the river was at one time a peninsula, at another an isolated island. The shore of this island, as well as the banks of the river adjoining the garden of Whist Bungalow, is densely overgrown with remarkable mangrove trees, whose peculiar land-producing activity I witnessed the first time I visited their neighborhood. The trees, which are comprised under the name of mangrove, or mangle-tree, belong to very various *genera* and families (*Rhizophora, Sonneratia, Lomnitzera, Avicennia*, etc.), but in their peculiar form of growth and consequent physiognomy they all essentially agree—a compact, usually circular, crown of foliage resting on a thick stem that rises from a mass of bare, interlaced roots. These dome-shaped root-works frequently rise above the surface of the water six or eight feet; the mud and sand from the surcharged rivers accumulate among them, and in this manner a clump of mangroves can materially favor an increase in the land. Many organic substances—dead bodies, fragments of animals and plants—also lodge in the interlaced roots, converting in many tropical localities, the mangrove-forest into a source of dangerous fevers. This, however, is not the case with the mangrove-forests of Ceylon, where the watered regions (for instance, the stagnant lagoons of Colombo) are by no means unhealthy. This, perhaps, may be accounted for by the fact that the copious and almost continuous rains on the island frequently renew the waters in the stagnant basins, and remove the decomposing substances before they effect any harm. Instead of mangroves there are a number of beautiful shrubs growing along the bank of our garden belonging to the *Asclepiadeæ* family (*Cerbera, Tabernæmontana, Plumiera*), all of them distinguished by clusters of large, white, deliciously-fragrant blossoms, like oleanders, hanging from the ends of the candelabra-like stem which rises from the centre of a shining tuft of dark-green leathery leaves. Most of these asclepia trees yield a poisonous milky sap. They belong to the most numerous and most characteristic decorations of the roadsides and swampy meadows of the richly-watered lowlands in the south-western part of the island. Between them, towering here and there above the bank, are huge but dainty tufts of the giant-grasses (*Bambusa*).

The garden proper of Whist Bungalow has, through the tasteful care of its proprietor, been converted into a charming bit of paradise in which may be found representatives of almost every important character-plant on the island; thus forming not only an odorous and flourishing pleasure garden, but an instructive botanic garden on a small scale. The first time I visited it and wandered, intoxicated with delight, among the palms and figs, bananas and acacias, I obtained an excellent idea of the plants comprised in the florâ of the lowlands. Naturally the first to deserve mention is the noble family of palms: cocoa and talipot, areca and borassus, caryota and Palmyra; then the splendid light green bananas with their delicate, wind-torn plumes and precious golden fruit. Besides the different varieties of the common banana (*Musa sapientum*), our garden contains a tall, magnificent example of the curious fan-shaped "traveler's-tree" of Madagascar (*Urania speciosa*). To the left of it is a fine specimen of the sacred fig tree (*Ficus bengalensis*), that, with its air-roots depending from the branches, some of them rooted in the ground, forms a very curious object; several graceful Gothic arches are formed by these root-trunks which act as supporting pillars for the main branches. Other trees, of various groups (terminalia, laurels, myrtles, iron-wood, bread-fruit, etc.), are overgrown and festooned by those lianas which play so important a part in the flora of Ceylon. These belong to various plant-families, for, in the midst of this unsurpassed plenitude of existence, under the matchless influence of perpetual heat and moisture, a multitude of different plants, growing in the dense thickets of this verdant wonder-island, climb upward by the aid of other plants to the light and air.

Other adornments in our charming garden are large-leaved callas, or *Aroideæ*, and graceful ferns—two plant-groups that play an important rôle in the lower flora of the island. Interspersed among the latter are many more ornamental foliage and flowering plants, some of which are indigenous to the island, and some from other regions of the torrid zone—namely, South America—but perfectly at home here. Above them tower stately hibiscus trees with large crimson or yellow flowers; flame-acacias (*Caesalpinia*) with huge, gorgeous, flame-colored nosegays; mighty tamarinds with aromatic blossoms, and, hanging in festoons from the branches, graceful thunbergias with huge violet bells; aristolochias with large yellow and brown trumpet-shaped blossoms. Of extraordinary size and gaudy coloring are many of the flowers of the madder plants (*Rubiaceæ*), lilies, orchids, etc.

But I shall not further impose on the reader meagre descriptions and uninteresting botanical terms in the vain hope that they will give him an adequate conception of the enchanting beauty unfolded by the Indian flora in Ceylon, and first seen by me in the garden of Whist Bungalow and on the banks of the Kalany River.

The first morning I spent in this paradise I wandered for hours intoxicated with delight from plant to plant, from tree-group to tree-group, unable to decide which of the countless wonders was most worthy of my attention. How paltry now seemed everything I had admired at Bombay!

The animal world which animates this Ceylon Paradise cannot compare in abundance or size with the extraordinary splendor and exuberance of the plant world.

In this respect the island, from what I have heard and read, cannot compare with the mainland of India, or the Sunda Islands.

It is also inferior to tropical Africa and Brazil, and I must confess that my first disappointment increased rather than diminished when I became familiar with the fauna of the more unfrequented portions of the island. I had hoped to find the trees and bushes covered with apes and parrots; the flowers with butterflies and beetles of rare forms and gorgeous hues. But neither the quantity nor quality of what I found came up with my extravagant expectations, and I had at length only the consolation of knowing that all the zoologists that had visited Ceylon before me must have experienced a similar disenchantment. However, careful search will reveal, even to the critical zoologist, much that is new and interesting; the fauna of Ceylon is after all no less original and curious, if not so abundant and beautiful, as its flora.

The vertebrates which from the very first most attracted me in the garden of Whist Bungalow and the neighborhood around Colombo, were numerous reptiles of brilliant hues and peculiar form, namely, snakes and lizards; pretty little tree-frogs (*Ixalus*) whose strange bell-like notes are heard everywhere in the evening.

Of the birds in the garden the most numerous are starlings and crows, water-wagtails, bee-eaters, and the dainty little creature which here takes the place of the humming-bird: the honey-bird (*Nectarinia*); king fishers, and herons are found along the banks of the rivers.

Of the mammals in the garden by far the most numerous are cunning little squirrels (*Sciurus tristriatus*) that scamper everywhere among the trees and bushes; they are very tame and trustful—are a brown-gray with three white streaks down their backs.

Among the insects, ants (from the most minute in size to the largest kinds) are the most preponderant; then termites or so-called "white ants." Other *Hymenoptera* (wasps and bees) as well as the *Diptera* are largely represented. On the other hand, those orders which include the largest and most beautiful forms — butterflies and beetles—are not as abundant as one would naturally expect from the exuberance of the vegetation. However, the *Orthoptera* (grasshoppers, crickets, etc.) are both curious and multiform.

Very interesting and remarkable articulates are offered by the spider class, or *Arachnida*, from the smallest mites and ticks to the gigantic bird-catchers and scorpions. The closely-allied milleped, or myriapod family is also largely represented; some of its members grow to an immense length—a foot long! and are greatly feared on account of their poisonous sting. I saw one of these colossal fellows the first morning in the garden at Whist Bungalow, but I had no time then to devote to animal-wonders,—my attention was too closely engaged with the beauty of the vegetable world. How gladly would I have devoted months and years to the study of this magnificent flora for which there were but a few short days and weeks at my disposal!

In addition to the attractions around me, the Indian sun shone so brightly in a deep blue, cloudless sky that my poor northern eyes were almost dazzled by the radiant light and brilliant hues, and the tropical heat would have been intolerable had there not been a cool gentle breeze from the sea. It was the 22d of November, the birthday of my dear father, who died ten years ago at the age of ninety. To-day he would have celebrated the one hundredth anniversary of his birth, and as my intense love for nature is an inheritance from him, a strangely solemn feeling came over me when I remembered what day it was, and I accepted the rare enjoyment of these precious hours as a fitting gift for this festal day!

Natural enjoyments like these have an inestimable value above all artistic and other pleasures in that they never pall, and that the nature susceptible to their influence ever returns to them with renewed sympathy and increased understanding. This is why the morning rambles in the paradisal garden of Whist Bungalow and the surrounding country—now along the banks of the river, now along the seashore—were repeated on every successive morning good fortune allowed me to remain in Colombo, and why I took leave of Ceylon, on the 10th of March, 1882, with a feeling of "Paradise Lost"! My botanical information was materially increased by several visits I paid to different English residents of Colombo and its suburbs. One visit in particular I remember with much pleasure. It was to the "Villa of the Temple-trees;" thus the plumiera trees are called because their large, deliciously fragrant flowers, together with the blossoms of the jasmine and the oleander, are scattered as offerings in front of the image of Buddha in the Buddhist temples. Two magnificent temple-trees, together with a gigantic casuarina, stood on the broad lawn which separated the stately villa from the Galle road. The proprietor of this handsome residence, Mr. Staniforth Green, had cordially invited me to spend several days with him. I found him a most agreeable old gentleman, and a most enthusiastic admirer of nature. Every hour he can spare from his extensive coffee-mills is devoted to the cultivation of a beautiful garden, and in collecting and studying the habits of insects and plants. With the sincere and passionate care which characterized the naturalist of the preceding century, and which is daily becoming more rare among the "assiduous" young "scientists" of the present day, Mr. Green has devoted years to studying the habits and development of the most minute insects, and has made a number of valuable discoveries, some of which have been published in the English newspapers.

He has a large number of exceedingly interesting curiosities, some of which he very kindly presented to me. His nephew, who is associated with him in business, is also devoted to this favorite study, and has a handsome collection of insects. From him also I received a number of gifts, among them several examples of the gigantic bird-catching spider (*Mygale*), whose chase after little birds (*Nectarinia*) and lizards (*Platydactylus*) Mr. Green has frequently observed.

Mr. Green's garden, which contains several ancient "flame acacias" (*Caesalpinia*), as well as some splendid yuccas and climbing palms (*Calamus*), lies on the banks of a charming little cove of the lagoon which extends between Colpetty, Slave Island, and the fort. One lovely evening we rowed across the cove, whose surface was spangled with exquisite white and red water-lilies, to the villa of Mr. William Ferguson. This amiable old gentleman (for many years superintendent of the construction of roads) also devotes his leisure hours to zoological and botanical researches, and has enriched those domains with a number of valuable contributions. To him also I am indebted for much interesting information. Mr. William Ferguson is not to be confounded with his totally dissimilar brother, the so-called "Ceylon Commissioner," the editor and publisher of the most influential newspaper on the island, the *Ceylon Observer*. This sheet is edited in that spirit of stern orthodoxy and intolerant bigotry which unfortunately distinguishes so many of the pretended "liberal"

English newspapers. At the time of my visit in Colombo the columns of the *Observer* were filled with a vigorous onslaught on a most meritorious and well-informed jurist, Mr. Berwick, a district judge, because he in one of his arguments had acknowledged and cleverly applied the Darwinian tenets of modern natural philosophy. The specific piety, however, of the "Ceylon Commissioner" did not hinder him from selling a faulty and unreliable map of the coffee district for eighteen rupees!

I accompanied Mr. Green to the Colombo Museum, an imposing two-storied building which stands in the Cinnamon Gardens, and contains collections of the literary, historical, and natural curiosities of the island. The lower story is occupied on one side by a valuable library, on the other are relics of antiquity: ancient inscriptions, sculptures, coins, ethnographic collections, etc. In the upper story is a rich collection of natural curiosities, principally dried and stuffed animals, exclusively Ceylonese. The insect family is especially rich in its representation—particularly those orders which Dr. Haly, the director of the museum, has made a special study. There is also a fine display of birds and reptiles, but in most divisions of the lower animal kingdom much still remains to be supplied. However, the exhibition of fauna peculiar to the island is very creditable, but the zoologist direct from Europe will find many of the specimens in a rather unsatisfactory condition. Many of the stuffed animals are badly prepared, mouldy, decayed, etc. But criticism of these faults will come only from the novice who is unfamiliar with the extraordinary difficulties which attend the preservation of such collections in the moist, hot-house climate of Ceylon. Bitter experience later convinced me of this fact. If in a perpetual heat of 20–25° R., and a moist atmosphere that surpasses the European conception of dampness, iron and steel rust in spite of every precaution, and leather and paper mould in a very short time, it is natural to suppose that the chitinous frames of insects as well as the skins of animals will sooner or later succumb to decay. Various insects also are as destructive as the heat and moisture: black and red ants (some of them two and three times as large as those at home, and some almost microscopic in size); white ants or termites (the worst of all insect enemies); giant cockroaches (*Blatter*), paper-lice (*Psocus*), wood-lice, and other vermin vie with each other in destroying a collection. Indeed it is almost impossible to protect anything destructible from the ceaseless attacks of these diminutive foes; in spite of every precaution I lost a large part of the collections I made while in Ceylon.

The first days of astonishment and admiration past, I began to unpack the thousand and one things in my trunks and boxes—and in what a condition I found most of them! Every particle of iron and steel about the scientific instruments was covered with rust; none of the screws would budge; every book, every bit of paper, as well as every article of leather, was damp and covered with mould. But what grieved me most was the condition in which I found my precious "dress-coat"—a garment that plays as important a rôle in English society here as at home in Europe. When I took it from the trunk I scarcely recognized it; it had completely changed color, and was, like all the rest of my wearing apparel, ornamented with landscapes executed in green and white mould! These vanished only after the garments had been aired and sunned for several days. Such a condition of affairs renders it absolutely necessary for every European household in Ceylon to employ a "clothes-boy," whose sole duty it is to prevent, by constant airing and sunning, the mould from accumulating on wearing apparel, household linen, paper, etc. The brand new photographic *camera obscura*, which I had purchased from a reliable house in Berlin, and which had been "warranted" made of "perfectly dry wood," was found on unpacking to be utterly useless; the wood was warped and twisted out of all shape, as were even the lids of my wooden boxes. The gummed envelops of which I had brought a supply were securely sealed; a box of pulverized gum-arabic had become a mass of solid cement, while a second box that I had filled with medicinal lozenges before leaving home contained a thick syrup strongly flavored with peppermint. Still more astonishing was the opening of a box of effervescent powders; the tartaric acid had vanished from the blue papers, while the white wrappers contained only some carbonate of soda instead of the original carbonic acid! This is what happened to me in Ceylon in the "dry season," from November to April; what must it be in the season called "wet" when, from May until October, the rain-teeming south-west monsoon prevails? My friends assured me that no one pretended to keep anything dry in the rainy season, and that the water ran down the walls.

That such a forcing-house temperature should uncomfortably affect the human organism accustomed to the totally different climate of Central Europe is very natural, also that the struggle with this inimical climate is the daily subject of conversation. I must confess that I was at a loss how to adapt myself to it. The first weeks in Colombo I found the annoyances and inconveniences almost unendurable, especially during the hot nights, when the temperature rarely fell below 20° R., while during the day it frequently rose in the shade to 24° and 28°. However the second week was not so disagreeable as the first, and later, even on the south coast near the fifth degree of south latitude, I never suffered as much as during the first sleepless nights and enervating days in Colombo. Under these conditions the daily bath becomes an indispensable luxury. I generally refreshed myself with three, one directly after rising in the morning about six o'clock, a second before the so-called "breakfast" at midday, and a third before dinner, about seven o'clock. I likewise adopted the peculiar dress worn by the Europeans in the tropics: garments made of the lightest cotton material, and a Calcutta or sola hat—an extremely light and comfortable covering for the head, made of the pith of the sola plant.

After adopting this costume, and strictly observing other precautionary regulations, which in the tropics are absolutely necessary for the preservation of health, I got on very comfortably, and was perfectly well during the entire time of my sojourn on the island, although—and perhaps too because I did so—I exercised every day, even during the hot hours of noon. Of course I lived more simply and abstemiously than is the custom here; I did not eat half the quantity of food, or drink half the amount the English resident considers necessary for his comfort. If these people, after a few years' sojourn in the tropics, complain of diseases of the liver and stomach, then the blame, according to my thinking, may be laid more to the want of proper exercise and the inordinate consumption of dainties than to the hot climate. Frequently they eat and drink three times as much, and of the richest food and hottest spirituous liquors, as is necessary for health. In this particular the habits of the English resident form a most decided contrast to those of the native, which are extremely simple; the food of the latter is chiefly rice and curry and several fruits, while his beverage is simply water, or at most palm wine.

In Ceylon, as in most parts of British India, the Europeans take their meals as follows: Mornings, directly after they arise, tea and biscuits, bread, eggs, marmalade, and fruits. At ten o'clock a breakfast that with us would be a complete dinner. The third meal "tiffin" follows at one o'clock. Many persons serve coffee and tea at three or four o'clock. At half past seven or eight, dinner—the principal meal—is served. Different wines accompany this meal, sherry, claret, champagne, and sometimes stronger liquors or beer which has been imported from England. Lately a better and lighter malt liquor from Vienna has taken the place of the English beer. In many houses one or two of these meals is dispensed with; but, as a general thing, the life of the foreigner in India is entirely too luxurious, especially when it is compared with the frugal habits of Southern Europe. This is also the opinion of several of the older English residents in Ceylon who lead simpler lives, and who, after an unbroken residence in the tropics of twenty or thirty years, still enjoy perfect health, as, for instance, Dr. Thwaites, the former excellent director of the Botanic Garden at Parcedenia.

V.

KADUWELLA.

THE many delightful experiences and noble impressions of my first week in Ceylon were crowned by a memorable excursion, in company with my friends, on the 27th of November, to Kaduwella. It was my first Sunday on the island, and, although the manifold enjoyments of the past week-days made every one of them seem a holiday, my festal mood attained its highest pitch on this my first extended tour into the more distant surroundings of Colombo, and, as the scenery of this part is essentially the same as that of the whole south west coast-land, I will attempt just here to give you a brief description of it.

Kaduwella is a strictly Singhalese village on the south bank of the Kalany River, ten English miles from Whist Bungalow. The excellent carriage road (which continues further to Awisawella and Fort Ruanwelle) now skirts the wooded banks of the Kalany, now crosses the country in wide detours to avoid the numerous windings of the river. Like all the carriage roads on the island this one is in perfect repair, a fact that is all the more deserving of praise when you remember that the violent and copious rains frequently wash out long stretches of the road, and render it an extremely difficult matter to maintain a highway in such excellent condition. But the English Government justly recognizes the importance of constructing and maintaining perfect media of communication in Ceylon as well as all the rest of her colonies; and it speaks volumes for her unequalled talent for colonization that, in order to accomplish her purpose—even in the face of almost insuperable difficulties—she spares neither expense nor labor.

My hosts from Whist Bungalow and several other German countrymen, who were living at the neighboring Elie House (once occupied by Sir Emerson Tennent), had made all the necessary arrangements for the gastronomic success of our excursion. All the solids and fluids requisite for an opulent breakfast *à la fourchette*, together with the firearms, ammunition, bottles, and tin-cases for my collections, etc., were packed in small, open caleshes drawn by a brisk Burmese pony, or else a stronger Australian horse. Almost all the carriage and riding horses' are imported from the mainland of India, or from Australia, as the practice of breeding horses is not successful in Ceylon. European horses, being unable to endure the climate, soon become useless. The little ponies from Burmah travel excellently well, although their powers of endurance are by no means great, ten miles (two or three hours) being sufficient to tire them out. The coachmen are usually Tamils clad in white jackets with red turbans; they display an astonishing amount of endurance as they run behind the calesh, or stand sideways on the step; they are obliged to keep up a continual hallooing, as the Singhalese (especially the aged people), together with their oxen and dogs, seem to have a decided predilection for being run over by a swiftly-traveling carriage.

The sun was not yet up when we drove away from Whist Bungalow, through the suburb of Mutwal and the contiguous grand pass, out into the smiling garden-land which, alternated by jungle, rice-fields, and meadows, stretches for miles to the foot of the mountains. The suburbs of Colombo, like those of all the cities on the island, extend imperceptibly, frequently for miles, into straggling villages along the road; and as each native hut is surrounded by a garden, a field, or a bit of woodland, it is often difficult to clearly define the limits of the separate villages. In the densely populated and richly cultivated portions of the flat coast-land there is no perceptible interruption, and one may say that the entire stretch of coast from Colombo to Matura,—the most southerly point of the island,—is occupied by a single, long village, interspersed with fruit-gardens, jungle, and cocoa-forest. Everywhere the same rustic elements characterize these paradisal gardens: picturesque brown earth-huts shaded by bread-fruit and mango trees, by cocoa and areca palms, garlanded by pisang hedges, ornamented with the gigantic foliage of the caladium and ricinus, the elegant papaya trees, manihot shrubs, and other useful plants.

On benches in front of the open huts the indolent Singhalese is stretched out in dreamy *dolce far niente*, engaged in lazily surveying his ever-green environments, or in leisurely searching for the tiny insect that infests the long black hair of his head. Naked children are playing everywhere, darting after the gaudy butterflies and lizards that animate the scene. At certain hours of the day numbers of ox-carts, single and double, are to be seen on the much-frequented road; these conveyances form the chief, indeed almost the only, means of transport and communication for the native population. The oxen belong to the zebu or Indian humped bison (*Bos indicus*) family, and are distinguished by a fleshy protuberance or hump on the shoulders. Like the bovine genera of Europe, the zebu family of India has many species; some of them—a diminutive species—are very swift and agile. Horses are rarely used by the natives, and asses are unknown to the island. Around the huts, everywhere, are large numbers of dogs (here called "pariah dogs"), all of the same species, ugly, bristly, brownish-yellow creatures, whose form, color, and disposition betray their jackal origin. Numbers of small, black hogs (*Sus indicus*) are also to be found everywhere; also long-legged lean goats; sheep are more rarely seen. There are numbers of chickens around the huts, but very few ducks and geese. These are the simple, ever-recurring elements which compose the village scenery of the whole south-west coast of Ceylon. But there is such a delicious naturalness about the simple components, they are grouped with such charming disregard for order and regularity and are of such infinite variety, they are illumined and tinted by the radiant tropical sunshine, the near seashore or river bank lends them fresh attractions, the background of forest, or distant mountain land, so much poetry, that one never tires admiring them, or thinking that the landscape and *genre* painter might here find a boundless wealth of exquisite subjects—subjects that are almost unknown to the art-exhibitions of the present.

A peculiarly charming effect of this Ceylonese coast landscape is the middle point which it seems to occupy between garden and forest scenery, between nature and cultivation. Often one imagines one's self in the midst of the most savage forest, encompassed by tall magnificent trees festooned and overgrown with lianas of all sorts. But a hut that lies quite in the shadow of a bread-fruit tree, a dog or a pig emerging from the bushes, playing children hiding under caladium leaves, tell us that we are only in a Ceylonese garden. On the other hand, the actual forest contiguous to the garden, with its multifarious combinations of the most different trees, its orchids, spice lilies, hibiscus, and other showy flowering plants, offers such a variety that we readily believe ourselves in a beautiful garden. This peculiar harmony between nature and cultivation is also expressed by the human life that animates these forest-gardens; the clothing and habitations of the Singhalese are of such primitive simplicity that the familiar descriptions of "genuine savages" might truthfully be applied to them, although they are descended from an ancient and cultured people.

All this is doubly attractive and picturesque in the early morning, when the rays of the sun are just beginning to peer through the interstices of the dewy foliage, when they cast long-drawn shadows of the slender stems and feathered crowns of the palms, and fling thousands of sparkling gems over the cloven leaves of the pisang.

During the time of my visit, at the period of the south-west monsoon, the morning hours were unfailingly clear and cloudless, and always refreshed by a deliciously cool and invigorating breeze from the sea, although the thermometer usually registered 20° R., rarely less than 18°. At nine or ten o'clock the heat increased and became oppressive; the sky was overcast by heavy storm clouds, which towards midday discharged copious showers. If these ceased by four or five o'clock then the evening was most delightful—especially if the setting sun flooded the clouds in the western sky with a radiance that defies all description. This year the rains were not as regular as in past years; there were also other exceptions to the general rule. On the whole, however, my excursions were usually favored by pleasant weather, and but few of my plans were frustrated by long-continued rains.

After a two hours' very interesting ride we arrived at the village of Kaduwella, which is picturesquely situated in a wide sweep of the Kalany River. Especially charming is the situation of the rest-house, under the shade of the most beautiful trees, on an eminence overlooking the river, at which we alighted and put up our ponies. Rest-house is the name given to the houses which the government, in the absence of hotels, has erected in Ceylon and India for the convenience of travelers, and which are under its control and management. In all Ceylon there are but three cities that can boast of a hotel: Colombo, Galle, and Kandy. The native does not require such houses of entertainment, consequently the foreign traveler is entirely dependent either on the hospitality of the European colonists (where there are such) or on the government rest-houses, which truly supply a most urgent need. The rest-house keeper, who is employed by the government, is obliged to furnish the traveler (for a small sum—usually a rupee—that is paid over to the government) with a room and a bed, as well as necessary food. Price and quality of the latter vary considerably, as also the condition of the rest-houses themselves.

In the south-western parts of Ceylon, where I spent most of my time, I found them generally good and very comfortable—particularly at Belligam, where I set up my laboratory in the rest-house for six weeks. But the reverse of good may be said of most of these government lodging-houses in many parts of the interior: in the northern and eastern parts of the island their accommodations are both inferior and expensive, as, for instance, in Neuera Ellia, where I had to pay for an egg a half, and for a cup of tea, a whole shilling. The rest-house at Kaduwella is one of the smaller and less pretentious lodging-houses, and as we had brought with us our own provisions, we required nothing from it but some chairs to sit on, water and fire to prepare our meal, and permission to eat it on the airy veranda, whose sheltering roof would protect us from the sun and rain, for all of which we were taxed accordingly.

In India nothing but death is gratuitous!

Shortly after our arrival we shouldered our guns and started out to take advantage of the beautiful morning. Behind the village, and to the south of the Kalany River, is a stretch of undulating country, over which our hunting party dispersed itself. The lower portions of this territory are covered with grass meadows and rice fields, intersected by numerous drains and canals, and adorned by miniature lakes, into which the latter empty. The elevations, gently-sloping hills from one to two hundred feet high, are clothed with dense jungle—and here I made my first acquaintance with this characteristic form of the landscape which on the whole island, wherever there is no cultivation, plays so important a part. The jungle cannot justly be called a "primeval forest," that is a region untrodden by the foot of man (in Ceylon such tracts are of small extent and rare occurrence); but it corresponds with our ideas of a primitive forest in that it, by its higher development, represents a forest form that is composed of a dense and impenetrable tangle of the most diverse varieties of trees. These have shot upward with a total disregard for regularity, unrestrained by human influence, and are so thickly overgrown with multitudes of creepers and climbing ferns, orchids, and other parasites, that it is quite impossible to disentangle the closely interwoven forms. That such a jungle, perfect in all its parts, is really impenetrable, unaided by fire and axe, my first attempt to enter it convinced me. A good hour's work enabled me to advance but a few steps into the thicket; then, utterly discomfited, I desisted from further attempt. I was stung by mosquitoes, bitten by ants, with torn clothing, bleeding arms and legs, wounded by the thousands of sharp thorns with which the calamus, hibiscus, euphorbias, lantanas, and a host of other jungle plants repulse every effort to penetrate their mysterious labyrinth. But my vain attempt was not entirely without reward. I not only became thoroughly familiar with the character of a jungle, with its splendid trees and lianas, I also beheld many new vegetable and animal forms that were of the greatest interest to me. I saw the magnificent *Gloriosa superba*—the poisonous climbing lily of Ceylon—with its red-gold chalices; the prickly *Hibiscus radiatus,* with huge sulphur-colored flower-cups, and hovering over them gigantic black butterflies with blood-red spots on their tail-shaped wing-appendages, and beetles that gleamed with a metallic lustre in the sunlight. But what delighted me most was, that on my first introduction to a Ceylon jungle I should also become acquainted with two of its most characteristic inhabitants —members of the highest animal class: apes and parrots. A flock of green parrots flew screaming from a tall tree that towered above the jungle when they saw my gun; and at the same time a number of large black apes fled chattering into the thicket. I did not succeed in getting a shot at either the former or the latter—they were evidently too familiar with the deadly effects of fire-arms. However, I was consoled by the fact that my first shot secured for me a colossal lizard, or iguana, over six feet long. This is the remarkable *Hydrosaurus salvator,* an animal much feared by the superstitious natives. The huge, crocodile-like beast was sunning himself on the edge of a ditch, and the first shot was so happily aimed at his head that instant death was the result; if the ball strikes a less vital part of the body the beast, which is very tenacious of life, will dart hastily into the water and disappear; with their powerful scaly tails they can defend themselves so effectively that a blow from them frequently causes serious wounds, sometimes even a broken limb.

After we had waded several ditches, and rambled some distance through a pleasant grove, we ascended a hill on which is a famous Buddhist temple, the object of numerous pilgrimages. We passed several groups of huts, which, half-hidden in the dense shade of mighty trees (terminalia and laurels), looked like so many toy-houses. Further on we crossed a sunny clearing, in which gorgeous butterflies and birds were flying about in great numbers, particularly woodpeckers and wild pigeons. At length a flight of steps between talipot palms led us up to the temple, which is in a rarely picturesque nook in the middle of a tall grove and under the shelter of a huge granite rock. A wide grotto that has evidently been enlarged by artificial means extends some distance beneath the overhanging mass of granite. The pillared hall of the temple is built into the grotto in such a manner that the naked rock not only forms the rear wall, but the material for the colossal image of the recumbent Buddha. The figure of the god is the same in all the Buddhist temples I visited while in Ceylon, as are also the monotonous paintings on the walls, which, in the interior of the temple, represent scenes from the earthly life of Buddha. These works of art, with their stiff, angular lines, and simple, harsh colors (principally yellow, brown, and red), remind one of the ancient Egyptian wall-paintings, although they differ materially in the details. The prostrate figure of Buddha, which rests on the right arm, and is enveloped in a yellow vestment, always exhibits the same staring and rigid expression, that reminds one of the forced smiles on the faces of the ancient Æginetan statues. Beside most of the Buddha temples is a dagoba, a bell-shaped dome without any opening, that is said to contain a relic of the god. The dagobas vary greatly in size, from that of a large church-bell to the circumference of the dome on St. Peter's at Rome. Near the dagoba there is usually a large ancient Bo-tree, or sacred fig tree (*Ficus religiosa*). In many parts of Ceylon these " Buddha trees," with their powerful trunks, fantastically interlaced roots, and huge crowns of foliage, form the most attractive features in the picturesque environs of the temples. The heart-shaped leaves on their long slender stems quiver like the foliage of our northern trembling aspen. A flight of granite steps behind the temple leads to the upper surface of the rock, from whence may be had a fine view of the neighboring hills and across the plain to the river. Palms and bananas adorn the immediate surroundings of the temple, and behind them an impenetrable thicket with lianas of all sorts forms a mystical background that fitly corresponds with the sanctity of the holy place. In front of the temple, on a rock beside the steps, crouched an old bald-headed priest in a yellow gown, and while I made a hasty sketch of him a Singhalese lad climbed a cocoa tree near, and fetched me one of its golden nuts; I found the sweetish, slightly acid water it contained a most refreshing drink for the hot noonday.

We returned to Kaduwella through a different part of the forest, and saw a number of new insects, birds, and plants; among the latter the celebrated teak tree (*Tectonia grandis*), as well as gigantic specimens of the cactus-formed wolfs-milk (*Euphorbia antiquorum*), with bare, blue-green prismatic branches. The latter part of our route, through swampy meadows, was so excessively hot that our first act on arriving at the rest-house was a plunge in the river—a delicious refreshment that gave the merry breakfast which followed a keener relish.

In the afternoon I rowed across the river to the thicket on the opposite bank, and found a number of plant-forms hitherto unknown to me—namely, *Aroideœ* and *Cannaceœ*. Along the banks of the river itself elegant bamboos alternating with terminalia, cedars, and mangroves, form the prevailing character of the forest.

It was late in the evening when, richly laden with zoological, botanical, and art treasures, we returned to Colombo. Afterwards I spent many more pleasant days in the jungles and along the river banks of Ceylon (and some of them were more beautiful than the banks at Kaduwella); but, as so often in life, the first impressions of new and strange objects are far more enduring, and not to be eclipsed by later superior attractions; consequently, the first day in the jungle of Kaduwella will ever remain a memorable event of my life.

VI.

PAREDENIA.

IN the central province of Ceylon, 1500 feet above the sea, lies the former capital of the island, the celebrated city of Kandy, and but a few miles distant from it Paredenia, a small town that for a brief season, five hundred years ago, likewise enjoyed the honor of being the regal residence of an ancient king. Here; in 1819, the English Government established a botanic garden, and entrusted Dr. Gardner with its management. His successor, Dr. Thwaites, the learned author of an excellent "*Flora Ceylonica*," for thirty years did everything in his power to raise the garden to a standard that would correspond with its peculiar climatic and local advantages. On his retirement, a few years ago, Dr. Henry Trimen was appointed director of the garden, and from this gentleman I received a cordial invitation to visit Paredenia. I accepted the kind invitation all the more readily, because I had already in Europe heard and read a great deal about the splendid collection of rare plants in the Botanic Garden of Paredenia, and my great expectations were not disappointed. If Ceylon is in truth a paradise for the botanist, as well as for every plant-friend, then Paredenia may justly be termed the heart of this botanical Eden.

Paredenia and Kandy are connected by a railway (the first in Ceylon) with Colombo, and the time necessary for a journey between the two termini is from four to five hours. At seven o'clock in the morning on the 4th of December I started from the Central Station in Colombo, and was in Paredenia by eleven o'clock. Like all true Europeans in Ceylon I had to travel first class ("*couleur blanche oblige*"). Only the yellow and brown "burghers and half-castes" travel in the second-class carriages, while those of the third class are occupied solely by the natives—the brown Singhalese and black Tamils. I was surprised not to find a fourth-class carriage for the latter, and a fifth for the despised "low castes." The natives, by the way, are very fond of railway travel, the only amusement on which they willingly expend much money. From the opening of the line to the present day many of the natives daily ride up and down the wonderful road, merely for the pleasure it gives them. The carriages are light and airy; those of the first class are furnished with excellent protection against the hot climate. The conductors and the white-clad, helmeted guards are English. Excellent order and punctuality reign here, as on all the lines managed by the British Government.

The first part of the journey from Colombo to Paredenia is across flat country, mostly covered with swampy jungle, alternated with rice fields and marshes. In the latter lie numbers of buffaloes, their black bodies half submerged in the water, while snowy herons carefully pick the insects from them. Farther on the line approaches the mountains, and at Rambukkana the ascent begins. The hours journey between this station and the one following, Kadugannava, is, as far as scenery is concerned, one of the most beautiful I have ever enjoyed. The line with many curves winds upward from the wide trough of the valley along the steep northern face of a rocky declivity. At first the eye is attracted by the manifold changes in the scenery of the immediate foreground; mighty blocks of gray gneiss rise above the exuberant masses of verdure which fill the narrow ravines on either side; lianas of most exquisite form hang from the tops of tall trees; charming little cascades leap merrily from points high above us; and, in the vicinity of the railway, we occasionally see the excellent public road, now so rarely used and once so frequently traversed, which the British Government built from Colombo to Kandy, and which only her enduring sway over the latter made feasible. Farther on the glance roves from the broad green valley expanding at our feet to the lofty mountain chain rising on the other side. Although the configuration of the highland mountains is, upon the whole, uniform, and not especially interesting (chiefly truncated cones of granite or gneiss), yet there are isolated peaks here and there which obtrude themselves on one's notice—as, for instance, the peculiar mass which bears the name of "Bible Rock." One of the grandest sights is obtained from "Sensation Rock," where the line, which has passed through several tunnels, beneath overhanging rocks, runs close to the very edge of a precipice that has a sheer descent of 1200–1400 feet. Roaring cascades leap from the rocky wall overhead, and dashing under the bridges of the line are transformed into veils of mist, bespangled with every tint of the rainbow, before they reach the emerald depths below.

The valley at our feet is covered partly with jungle and partly by cultivated land, over which are scattered numerous huts, gardens, and terraced rice fields. Everywhere above the lower shrubbery tower the giant stems of the mighty Palmyra palms (*Corypha umbraculifera*), the proud queen among the palms of Ceylon. Its perfectly upright stem resembles a slender white marble column, and frequently grows to a height of over one hundred feet. Every one of the fan-shaped leaves composing the ponderous crown would cover a half-circular space sixteen feet in diameter—a superficial area of two hundred square feet; they, like every part of the tree, are used for various purposes, principally for thatching; they are specially celebrated, however, for their being formerly employed by the Singhalese as a substitute for paper, and are still used as such for many purposes. The ancient "Puskola" manuscripts in the Buddha monasteries were written with an iron style on "ola" paper—narrow strips of talipot leaves boiled in water and dried. The talipot blooms but once during its life, usually between its fiftieth and eightieth years. The stately pyramid of bloom in the centre of the leaf-crown frequently reaches a length of thirty or forty feet, and is composed of millions of small creamy blossoms; when the nuts have ripened the tree dies. I was fortunately favored with the rare sight of an unusual number of talipot palms in bloom; between Rambukkana and Kadugannava I counted over sixty, and along the entire line over one hundred. Numerous excursions were made from Colombo to view the magnificent spectacle.

On the pass of Kadugannava, nearly 2000 feet above the sea, the railway as well as the neighboring public road reach their highest point; a monument commemorating the services of Captain Dawson, builder of the latter road, has been erected here. This pass is also a watershed. The numerous streams we saw threading the green velvet valley like so many strands of silver, flow either into the Kalanyganga or the Maha-oya, both of which debouch on the sea from the west coast. Those streams on the eastern slope of the Kadugannava flow into the Mahawelli-ganga, the largest river on the island, which is 134 miles long, and flows into the sea from the east coast at Trincomalie. Along the banks of the latter stream, beside which extend plantations of sugar-cane, the train brought us in a quarter of an hour to Paredenia, the last station before Kandy. When, at eleven o'clock, I arrived at Paredenia I found Dr. Trimen awaiting me; after a cordial welcome he drove me in his carriage to the Botanic Garden, a mile distant from the railway station. Just before reaching the Garden, we crossed the foaming river on a beautiful bridge of satinwood, with a single span of two hundred feet. When the water is at its usual level, the highest point of this span is seventy feet above the river; and some idea may be formed of the enormous bulk of water that surcharges the rivers of Ceylon after a heavy rain, when one learns that during these periods the bridge is but from ten to twenty feet above the flood—the water having risen from fifty to sixty feet.

The entrance to the garden is through an avenue of noble india-rubber trees (*Ficus elastica*). This is the tree whose inspissated milk-sap forms the caoutchouc of commerce, and whose young plants are frequently seen in the greenhouses of our rugged north. While these india-rubber plants with us are objects of admiration when their slender stems grow to the height of the ceiling, and their few branches bear from fifty to one hundred leathery, egg-shaped leaves, here in their hot mother-country they develop into gigantic trees of the highest rank, and rival our proudest European oaks. The immense crown of many thousands of leaves covers with its mighty branches (40–50 feet long) the superficial surface of a stately palace, while from the base of the thick trunk extends a net-work of roots that frequently measures from one hundred to two hundred feet in diameter—far more than the height of the tree itself. This astounding root-crown consists mostly of twenty or thirty main roots, from each of which branch as many more—all of them curving and twisting over the ground like so many gigantic serpents, for which reason the Singhalese call it the "snake-tree," and poets at various times have likened it to the snake-entwined Laocoön. The spaces between the roots form veritable closets or sentry boxes, in some of which a man standing upright may effectually conceal himself. Similar root-columns are developed by other large trees of different orders.

Scarcely had I expressed my admiration for this avenue of snake-trees, when my eyes were enchained by another wonderful sight near the garden gate. There, as if to greet the new-comer, stood a huge bouquet of palms, composed of those species indigenous to the island, and a number of foreign representatives of this noblest of tropical families; garlands of lovely creepers festooned their crowns, while their stems were ornamented with the most exquisite parasitic ferns. A similar but handsomer and more extensive group stands near the end of the main alley, and is encircled by a lovely wreath of flowering plants. Here the alley branched, the path on the left leading to a slight eminence on which stands the bungalow of the director. This enviable home is, like most Ceylonese villas, a low, one-storied structure, encircled by an airy veranda whose wide, projecting roof is supported by a row of white pillars. Roof and pillars are adorned with luxurious vines, large-flowered orchids, odorous vanilla, showy fuchsias, and other bright flowers; choice collections of flowering plants and ferns embellish the garden beds which surround the house, and above them rise the shade-dispensing crowns of India's noblest trees. Numerous gorgeous butterflies and beetles, lizards and birds animate this charming picture.

As the villa stands on the highest eminence in the garden, and the broad, velvety lawn slopes away from it on every side, the view from the veranda embraces a large portion of the garden with several of its most attractive tree-groups, and the belt of tall forest trees which encloses the meadow land. Beyond them rise the wooded summits of the mountain chain which encircles Paredenia valley.

The Mahawelli-ganga flows in a wide, semi-circular sweep around the garden, and separates it from yonder chain of hills; consequently it lies on a horseshoe-shaped peninsula whose land side, where it adjoins the Kandyan valley, is effectually protected by a tall, impenetrable hedge of bamboo, thorny rattan, and other equally formidable plants. As the climate (at 1500 feet above sea level) is extraordinarily favorable, and the tropical heat of the sheltered valley, in conjunction with the copious rains which fall in the neighboring mountains, transform the Paredenia Garden into a natural forcing-house, it will be readily understood that the tropical flora here develops her wonderful productive power in the highest degree. My first ramble through the garden, in company with the well-informed director, convinced me that this was indeed the case; and although I had read and heard so much about the wonderful attractions of the exuberant tropical vegetation, had longed for so many years to behold it with my own eyes, the actual reality, the actual enjoyment of the fabled glories, far surpassed my highest expectations, and that, too, after I had been prepared by what I had seen in Bombay and Colombo. In the four days I spent at Paredenia I gained more information concerning the life and habits of the plant world than I could have acquired at home in as many months by the most diligent botanical study. And when, two months later, I returned to the garden for a farewell visit, my delight was as great as when I first beheld its manifold attractions. I cannot adequately express my gratitude for the courteous hospitality and wealth of information I received from my good friend, Dr. Trimen; the seven days in his enchanting bungalow were, for me, seven veritable days of creation!

At the time of my visit in Paredenia there was also another English botanist there—Dr. Marshall Ward—who had finished his studies in Germany, and whose official title was "Royal Cryptogamist." He had been sent here by the English Government to investigate the "coffee-leaf disease"—the formidable fungus disease of the leaves of the coffee tree, which for years has been ravaging with increasing violence on the coffee plantations, destroying large numbers of this most valuable plant, and a most profitable source of revenue to the national treasury. Dr. Ward has made a number of important observations and experimental investigations of the disease, and has fully elaborated the natural history of the microscopic, rust-like fungus (*Hemileja vastatrix*); but he was unfortunately unable to discover a radical cure for it. In gratitude for his wearisome labors he is sharply assailed by the press—especially by many of the coffee planters! As if the hundreds of naturalists in Europe, who are engaged in studying similar fungus epidemics, always succeeded in finding a remedy for a disease directly they became familiar with its character! Such is rarely the case; and among the many absurd opinions which are daily promulgated in our "cultured circles," certainly one of the most absurd is that "for every disease there must be a remedy." The experienced physician and naturalist, who is familiar with the actual facts, knows that this is of rarest occurrence, and is disposed rather to wonder that a radical remedy exists for certain diseases—as, for instance, cinchona for fever.

It would only weary the indulgent reader, were I to vainly attempt, without the aid of illustrations, to introduce him to the botanical Eden of Paredenia. Nor would the numerous water-color sketches and drawings I made while there materially assist me. I shall therefore restrict myself to a few general observations, and the notice of several of the most important plant-forms. Vastly unlike most of the botanic gardens of Europe, whose stiff rows of beds remind one of files of soldiers, the Paredenia garden (150 acres) is arranged with regard to æsthetic effect as well as for the systematic classification of the plants. The principal tree-groups, and plants of kindred species, are tastefully distributed over grassy lawns, with pleasant paths leading from one to the other. In a more retired part of the garden are the less attractive beds for the cultivation of useful plants. Almost all of the useful plants of the torrid zone (of both hemispheres) are here represented; seeds, scions, and fruits of many of them are annually distributed among the planters and gardeners on the island. Thus the garden is not only an experimental station and acclimatization garden, but it has for years conferred important practical benefits on the colonists.

The singularly favorable climatic and topographical conditions under which the garden flourishes would also admirably adapt it to the purely scientific experiments of a *botanic station*. In a like manner, as our young zoologists are able to prosecute their scientific studies in the lately established zoological stations along the sea-coast (at Naples, Roscoff, Brighton, Triest, etc.), so the student of botany might in one year learn more in the botanic station of Paredenia than he could possibly accomplish in ten at home. As yet the tropical zone, the richest in material for botanical study, contains no such institution. If the English Government were to establish and support a botanic station at Paredenia, and a zoological station at Galle (for instance, in Captain Bayley's charming and admirably adapted bungalow), she would add to the important services she has already rendered to science by the *Challenger* expedition and other similar scientific undertakings; she would again shame the continental states of Europe that have no money to expend for anything but breech-loaders and cannon!

If, among the many wonders in Paredenia Garden only a few are to be briefly noticed, then I shall begin with the celebrated giant bamboos, the astonishment and admiration of every visitor. Rambling from the entrance gate towards the river and along its lovely bank, we see, while still at a distance, huge green bushes over one hundred feet high, and as many broad, which spread their plumed heads—like the feather brushes of giants—high above the river and the road, casting delightful shadow over both. Approaching nearer we see that this stupendous mass of verdure is composed of numerous (from 80 to 100) slender stems from one to two feet thick, which have sprung from a common root, and bear, on delicate, nodding branches, dense clusters of the daintiest leaves. And these gigantic trees are nothing but grasses! Like all grass stalks these prodigious tubes are jointed; but the sheath which, in the delicate species, is a thin, small scale at the base of the leaf, is, in this bamboo giant, a firm woody partition that, without further preparation, might serve as a shield for the breast of a vigorous man. A child of three years might hide in one of the joints! As is well known, the bamboo belongs to the useful plants of the tropics; but to fully describe the manifold uses to which these tree-grasses—as well as the palms—are turned to account by the natives would fill a whole volume.

Next to the bamboos—or, indeed, before them—come the palms. Beside the orders indigenous to the island, we find here a number of palms that are natives of the mainland of India, the Sunda Islands, Australia, and tropical America—as, for instance, the *Livistonia chinensis*, with its huge crown of fan-shaped leaves; the celebrated *Lodoicea* from the Seychelles, with its colossal fans; the

Elæis, or oil-palm of Guinea. with its long, plume-like foliage; the famous *Mauritia* from Brazil; the lofty *Oreodoxa*, or king's-palm, from Havana, etc. Of the latter I admired and sketched, on Teneriffe (1866), a splendid specimen, and was therefore not a little surprised and delighted to behold here a whole avenue of the stately trees. No less interesting were splendid groups of thorny climbing palms or rattans (calamus) with delicate, vibrating leaves; their slender but firm and elastic stems climb to the tops of the highest trees, often attaining a length of three or four hundred feet. They belong to the longest of all plants.

But one must pay a penalty for wandering among palms. While rambling through the tall grass on the river bank, beneath the giant crown of an oil-palm, my fascinated gaze following the windings of an ambitious rattan, I suddenly felt several sharp stings on my leg; an examination revealed a pair of diminutive leeches that had attached themselves to me, while half a dozen or more of their fellows were nimbly ascending the leg of my boot. This was my first introduction to the notorious land-leech of Ceylon, the most annoying of all the numerous plagues on this beautiful island. This species (*Hirudo ceylonica*) belongs to the smallest, as well as the most disagreeable of the genera. With the exception of the sea-coast and the higher mountain country, they are found in the greatest profusion everywhere on the island—especially on the banks of the rivers and in the damp jungles of the lowland hills, where one cannot take a step without being attacked by them. They not only creep along the ground, but infest the bushes and trees, from whence they drop on the unsuspecting passer-by; they will even make a sudden jump to reach their prey. When fully distended the land-leech is as large as the smaller medicinal leeches; before his feast, however, he is about half an inch in length, scarcely thicker than a thread, and penetrates the heaviest stocking with amazing rapidity. Frequently their sting is immediately felt, and very often not. Once, in an evening company, I was made aware of their presence only when I saw the blood trickling down the leg of my white pantaloons.

To prevent an attack from these pests a drop of lemon juice is sufficient, for which reason a small lemon is always carried in the pocket when rambling in the lowlands. Instead of this remedy, however, I made use of carbolic acid, or alcohol, both of which I always carried with me on my collecting tours. The effects of their sting are very different. Persons with sensitive skins (to which class I unfortunately belong) suffer for several days from an annoying irritation, and not infrequently the wound is attended by more or less painful inflammation. As the leeches prefer these tender, inflamed parts, the wounds very frequently become quite serious. When the English, in 1815, conquered Kandy, and the ›troops were obliged for weeks to force their way through the jungles, many soldiers were lost by the incessant attacks of these minute leech foes. In the regions where they are most numerous, the Europeans are obliged to wear leech-gaiters made of rubber or closely woven cloth, which are drawn over the boot and fastened around the knee. Always when starting for the jungle I took the precaution to smear a streak of carbolic acid around the tops of my hunting boots. In some parts of the island these leeches, by their enormous number, render—as do the ticks (*Ixodes*) in other parts—a stay of any length almost impossible. Another diminutive plague in the garden of Paredenia (as in all watered regions on the island) is the musquito and stinging fly; musquito nets for the bed-chambers are an absolute necessity. But far more dangerous than these insects, which are only troublesome pests, are the poisonous scorpions and millepeds of which I secured some splendid examples.

One of the most attractive parts of Paredenia is the fern garden. In the dense shade of tall trees along the cool banks of a murmuring brook is assembled a company of small and large, delicate and vigorous, herbaceous and arboreous ferns, such as it would be impossible to imagine any more charming and agreeable. The entire charm of form which distinguishes the dainty feathery foliage of our native ferns is here displayed in an endless variety of different species, from the simplest to the most complex; and while some of the pretty little dwarf ferns might easily be confounded with dainty mosses, the giant tree-ferns, whose slim, black stems bear a lovely crown of feathery leaves, attain the proud height of the palm.

Like the ferns, the fern-palms, or *Cycadeæ*, as well as the dainty selaginella and lycopodia families, are represented in Paredenia by choice collections of the most interesting species, from the most minute, moss-like forms to the robust shrub sorts that almost remind one of the extinct tree-lycopodia of the stone-coal period. Indeed, many plant-groups in this garden recall to mind the fossil flora so admirably portrayed by Unger in his views from an antidiluvian world.

If, in conclusion, but two more plant orders, which are of peculiar interest to me, are to be introduced to your notice, then the first shall be the lianas, and the second the banyans. Although creeping and climbing plants are abundant everywhere on the island, the Paredenia Garden contains several splendid examples, the like of which are rarely found; for instance, colossal vines of the *Vitis, Cissus, Puriada, Bignonia, Ficus*, etc. Also the banyans, and several kindred fig trees (*Ficus galaxifera*, etc.), are the finest, most magnificent tree-forms I saw on Ceylon.

A very remarkable sight was presented by one of these ancient banyan trees, whose mighty crown rested on numerous root-columns; it was almost entirely denuded of foliage, but large numbers of what seemed to be a monstrous brown fruit hung from the bare branches. Imagine my astonishment when, on approaching the tree, several of these "fruits" suddenly took wing and flew away! They were flying foxes (*Pteropus*), of that remarkable group of frugivorous bats which is confined to the tropical zone of the old world (Asia and Africa). Several cleverly-aimed shots brought half a dozen to the ground, whereupon the rest of the flock (several hundred) flew loudly screaming away. Those of the fallen that had only been wounded vigorously defended themselves with their sharp teeth and claws, and it was only after considerable difficulty that I succeeded— with the aid of my hunting knife—in conquering them. These "flying foxes" are, in shape—especially the head—size, and color very similar to the fox. But the limbs, like those of all other bats, are connected by a tough wing-membrane that enables them to fly very swiftly. Their motion is very different from that of our northern bats; it is more like the flight of a crow. They feed on fruits, and are therefore very destructive. They are particularly fond of the sweet palm wine, and are often found by the natives in a tipsy condition in the sap vessels hanging on the palms. This propensity sufficiently explains the near consanguinity which the phylo-genetic genealogy of the mammalia establishes between them and the apes—likewise man!

In the sorrel-hued fur of the flying fox I found large parasitic insects (*Nycteribia*) of peculiar, spider-like form, belonging to the *Pupipara* group. These insects—like the fleas—are *Diptera*, or flies, which, in consequence of parasitic habits, have ceased to fly, and through disuse of their wings have eventually become wingless insects. However, they can travel with surprising activity over the bodies of their hosts—also over my hand, as I found when I tried to capture some of them. Several particularly nimble fellows disappeared up my sleeve and buried their sharp claws in my flesh.

That same day I made another interesting but dangerous zoological acquaintance. While engaged, during a rain storm in the afternoon, in imprisoning a gigantic black myriapod in a spirit bottle, a large hooded snake, the dreaded *Cobra di capello* (*Naja tripudians*), crept through the open garden door into my bedroom. I had not noticed him, although he was scarcely a foot away from me, and became aware of his presence only when my servant dashed, excitedly shrieking "Cobra! cobra!" into the room. With the native's assistance I soon mastered the poisonous monster (he was over a metre in length), and he now occupies a spirit bottle in company with a remarkable snake-like amphibia, *Cæcilia*, I found a few days before.

VII.

KANDY.

AMONG the few cities Ceylon can boast Kandy, although it can scarcely be called a city, enjoys a distinct and separate reputation; partly from its being the capital of the central province, partly because it was once the residence of the native Kandyan kings, and partly because an ancient temple in its precincts contains the "sacred tooth" of Buddha, one of the most celebrated relics of this religion.

In addition to these attractions I had read in Sir Emerson Tennent's excellent work on Ceylon, a glowing description of Kandy's incomparably beautiful situation and environs— enthusiastic praise that was echoed by later travelers who, in their descriptions, usually imitated Sir Emerson. Consequently, the expectations with which I set out from Paredenia on the morning of the 6th of December for the three miles distant Kandy were by no means small.

So often in my travels I have found that the world-famed places, which it is the "fashion" to visit, and whose praise every tourist feels it incumbent upon himself to repeat, were, in fact, scarcely worth visiting; while frequently there would be in close juxtaposition really charming neighborhoods which were wholly ignored by the tourist because they were not mentioned in the "guide-books." This was again my experience in Ceylon with the far-famed city of Kandy, and I shall, without further preamble, at once confess that my visit here was, from beginning to end, a huge disappointment.

The "proud regal city" might better pose as an "unpretending village," whose few streets contain more Singhalese earth-huts than European bungalows, and these dwellings are not even divided—as in Colombo, Galle, Matura, and other cities on the island—into a "white town," or fort, and a "black town," or *pettah*. Two long parallel streets are crossed at right angles by a few smaller ones; the "lovely lake" which lies in front of the city, and which is extolled as a peculiar embellishment, is a small artificial pond of rectangular shape, whose banks are flanked by perfectly straight rows of trees. If, therefore, you rise above the little valley which contains Kandy and its lake, and ascend one of the numerous artificial "walks" to the summit of one of the surrounding hills, the view is excessively stiff and artificial, and anything but picturesque. It is further disfigured by a large, lately-built prison, with high bare walls, that is much too large and massive for the proportions of its surroundings. Nor were the partly-cultivated, partly-wooded hills which encircle the valley, and above which rise several taller ranges, specially attractive, either in beauty of outline or picturesque grouping. This will explain why the sketch-book I took with me to Kandy with the best of intentions remained blank; I was unable to find a single point that was worth perpetuating in water-colors.

Kandy's principal beauty—to my taste at least—is the lovely garden which surrounds the modern palace of the governor. It is tastefully laid out on the slope of a hill, and contains, in addition to a great many fine trees, a number of ornamental plants. But it is not to be compared with the Paredenia Garden. The palace itself, in which, invited by the governor, I spent a very pleasant evening, contains but a few large airy apartments; they are elegantly furnished, and open on the veranda. Multitudes of snakes, scorpions, and other tropical vermin are said to render a sojourn here anything but agreeable and comfortable.

The so-called "palace" of the ancient Kandyan kings stands on the banks of the lake, and is a low, gloomy-looking structure whose dark, musty interior contains nothing of special interest except the dense masses of fungi, and other cryptogams, which completely cover the thick damp walls inside and out. Near by is the "Royal Audience Hall," supported by carved pillars; it is used at present as the district court-house.

Nor does the celebrated "Buddha Temple of Kandy," which, together with the ancient palace, is enclosed by a high wall and surrounded by a moat, fulfil the expectations naturally aroused by its wonderful reputation. It is of inconsiderable dimensions, badly preserved, and without any artistic merit whatever. The primitive wall paintings, as well as the carved ornaments of wood and ivory, are the same as those in other Buddhist temples. As Kandy was not elevated to the dignity of a regal residence until towards the close of the 16th century, and the palace, as well as the temple, were not built until 1600, the city cannot claim even the charm of great antiquity. Very little real interest is connected with the famous "sacred tooth," which is kept under a silver bell in an octagon tower of the temple. Although this tooth has, for more than two thousand years, been devoutly worshipped by many millions of superstitious people, and although it plays an important part in the history of Ceylon, it is, after all, but a simple, rudely-carved piece of ivory, about two inches long and one thick. There is a "true Buddha tooth" in several localities, but this does not impair the sanctity of any one of them.

In company with my two botanical friends, Drs. Trimen and Ward, I paid a visit to "Fairyland," the residence of Dr. Thwaites, the former director of the Paredenia Botanic Garden. His enchanting bungalow is quite hidden in a ravine among the mountains, about eight miles south of Kandy, and is surrounded by coffee plantations.

Dr. Thwaites is the meritorious author of a work on the flora of Ceylon that appeared in London (1864) under the title of *Enumeratio Plantarum Zeylanica*. In it he describes upward of three thousand phænogamic plants indigenous to the island, one thirtieth part of all the plants then known on the globe. Since then, however, many new ones have been discovered, and, according to the estimate of Dr. Gardner, there are in Ceylon nearly 5000 species, a considerably larger number than all Germany can produce. The *Flora of Ceylon* which I had brought with me, formerly belonged to a German botanist named Nietner. He came to Ceylon a young gardener, had by thrift and industry become the owner of a valuable coffee plantation, and had, for a quarter of a century, taken an active interest in the natural history of the island, and discovered a number of new insects. He died, unfortunately, before he could return to his native land. His widow, who lives in Potsdam, and who, before I sailed for India, gave me some valuable information and advice, presented me with several of her husband's books, among them a copy of Dr. Thwaites's *Flora* that had been presented to Mr. Nietner by the author himself. The worthy old gentleman was greatly pleased when I showed him the book. It was doubtless the first copy of his work that had been carried from Ceylon to Europe by a botanist and back again by a zoologist.

VIII.

The Galle-Colombo Road.

My first two weeks in Ceylon passed in continual sight-seeing and wonderment like a dream.

In Colombo I had become acquainted with the most important characteristics of the Singhalese human and natural worlds, had admired in Paredenia the astounding productive power of the tropical flora. It was now time to think of the scientific motive of my journey, the investigation of the multiform and, to some extent, unknown Indian marine animals.

I was particularly anxious to resume, on the shores of Ceylon, the study of those animal classes in which I have been interested for a number of years, such as mollusks, radiolarians, sponges, corals, medusæ, and siphonophora, for I expected to find here entirely new forms, developed under the influence of the tropical sun and the Indian conditions of life.

The conditions under which these marine animals attain their highest development are manifold and peculiar; and it is by no means immaterial what part of the coast we select for their investigation. The perfect development of the marine fauna depends not only on the quality of the sea-water—its saltness, purity, temperature, current, and depth, but also (and frequently to a considerable extent) on the configuration of the contiguous shore, whether it be rocky or sandy, calcareous or slaty, whether fertile or barren. Again, the existence of certain groups is favored, or hindered, by the quantity of fresh water that flows into the ocean, and by the force of the surf on the shore. For the development of those divisions of swimming animals in which I am specially interested—radiolarians, medusæ, and siphonophera—the most favorable regions are the deep land-locked bays with clear, still water, sheltered by rocky projections, undisturbed by large volumes of fresh water, and supplied with currents that lead the pelagic fauna into them. To favorable conditions like these the harbor of Messina, the Gulf of Naples, and Bay of Villafranca, in the Mediterranean, owe the reputation they have won in the last decade among zoologists.

A glance at the map of India will show that such sheltered bays are of rarer occurrence along its coast than along the dented shores of our matchless Mediterranean. On the coast of Ceylon there are but three such bays: the picturesque harbors of Galle and Belligam on the south-west coast; and the celebrated island-adorned Gulf of Trincomalie on the north-west coast. The latter was declared by Nelson one of the finest harbors in the world. The English Government, which is quick to see and improve the natural advantages of her possessions, lost no time after the acquisition of Ceylon in fortifying Trincomalie. The Dutch had already erected forts on each of the two tongues of land projecting into the harbor: Fort Frederick on the northernmost, and Fort Ostenburg on the southern. These were enlarged and strengthened by the English, and many other improvements made in the little town. But much still remains to be done, especially when it is remembered that Trincomalie is the most important harbor of defence in all British India. In the struggle for the possession of India, in which the British empire will, sooner or later, have to participate, this fortified harbor will, as may easily be seen, play an important part.

The harbor of Trincomalie, distinguished not only for its size and depth, but for its picturesque shores and numerous wooded islands which guard its entrance, leads one from the very first to expect a peculiarly rich development of marine animal life. And, indeed, many groups of sea-creatures, particularly those that frequent a rocky bottom (mollusks and echinoderms) here seem to unfold a larger number of different sorts than most points along the coast. It is specially famous for its wealth of conchylia: beautifully tinted snails, and delicately fashioned mussels. Several zoologists who have visited Trincomalie have discovered some entirely new animal forms. It was, therefore, natural that I should turn my attention to this point in preference to all others, and conclude to fish at least a month among its productive waters. But, when it came to carrying out my plans, insurmountable difficulties presented themselves. Communication between Trincomalie and the rest of the larger towns on the island is still very imperfect, and leaves much to be desired, by water as well as by land. As yet, nothing has been done toward the projected railway between Kandy and Trincomalie. As the former city lies almost midway between the west and east coasts, and has for years been connected by rail with Colombo, the continuation of the line to the east coast would seem almost a necessity, especially when we consider the strategic importance of Trincomalie and the superiority of her harbor, which, in a commercial sense, is but little used. At present the journey from Kandy to Trincomalie, is over a wretched road that for days leads through uninhabited forests. At the time I thought of making the journey, in the beginning of December, the condition of the road was particularly uninviting; the heavy rains of the south-west monsoon had swept away several bridges, and rendered long stretches of the road almost impassable. I was afraid the bullock carts on which my sixteen chests of instruments, etc., would have to be transported to Trincomalie, would either stick fast in the mud, or reach their destination under great difficulties in a damaged condition. The prospects by sea were no brighter. The little government coast-steamer, the *Serendib*, which makes semi-monthly trips around the island, forms the only regular and direct communication between the principal points on the coast; the sailing vessels plying between these ports are neither safe nor reliable. As ill luck would have it, just at the time I wanted to engage passage on the *Serendib* for Trincomalie she was damaged in a storm, and towed to Bombay for repairs. Consequently I was forced to postpone my visit, and later, further hindrances compelled me, much to my regret, to renounce the plan altogether.

There was now nothing left for me to do but to seek the south-west coast, and set up my zoological laboratory either at Galle or Belligam. Galle, or Point de Galle, the most prominent seaport on the island, which, until within a few years, was the principal station for all the Indian vessels, and the usual place of debarkation for European travelers, offered me the advantages of European civilization, facilities for procuring what I might require, and constant intercourse with cultured English residents. I might there count to a certainty on fishing in a large, beautiful harbor from European boats, on finding among the celebrated coral banks a wealth of interesting sea animals, and on examining and preserving them with proportionate ease and convenience. There were still other advantages: other zoologists had visited Galle before me, and by their discoveries had facilitated my acquaintance with its locality and animal life. Ransonnet's handsome book in particular, contains a number of important observations on the Galle coral banks. Very different conditions awaited me at Belligam. True, the lovely sheltered bay at this place, fifteen miles south of Galle (half way between the latter port and Matura, the most southerly point of the island), could boast of coral banks and other topographical and zoological conditions very similar to those of Galle, and it had besides, owing to its being rarely visited or explored, the great charm of novelty, and of being comparatively unknown. . From what I had heard, Belligam surpassed Galle in beauty of scenery and exuberant vegetation. But what charmed me even more than this was, that in the former place I might for several months throw off the conventionalities and unnaturalness of our civilized world, and, in the midst of tropical nature's wanton luxuriance, for once yield myself to the full enjoyment of its beauties. Here, surrounded by a simple, uncultured people, I might hope to gain an idea of the imaginary paradisal condition of our primitive ancestors. For Belligam is in reality nothing but a large, purely Ceylonese village, inhabited by fishermen, shepherds, and tillers of the soil; its four thousand chocolate-hued inhabitants, among whom there is not a single European, live partly along the picturesque shores of the bay, and partly on a lovely level stretch of cocoa-forest that verges on the shore. In Belligam's secluded rest-house I might hope to accomplish more work, and with more coherence and dispatch than in sociable Galle, surrounded by many kindly-disposed friends and inquisitive acquaintances.

After maturely considering its advantages and disadvantages, I at last decided in favor of Belligam, and had no reason afterwards to regret my choice. The six most fruitful weeks I spent there will ever remain a memorable period; they form one of the choicest flower-groups in the garland of my Indian reminiscences. I might have found Galle more convenient for my special zoological study, but, for a general view of nature and of nature's people Belligam was the better place.

Naturally there were numerous preparations to be made for a protracted sojourn in this isolated fishing-village. As lodgings were to be had only in the government rest-house, and the traveler's stay in these substitutes for hotels is restricted to three days, it was necessary to obtain permission to occupy the rest-house at Belligam for several months. The governor of Ceylon, Sir James Longdon, to whom I brought letters from the English Government (and to whom I am indebted for many courtesies), furnished me with letters to the president of the south province. In them not only the desired permission was granted, but several government officials were ordered to render me any service I might require. With the exemplary order and discipline which attends the governmental mechanism in the English colonies, as well as in the mother-country, an official document like this is at times an indispensable talisman. Especially is this the case in Ceylon, as the island is entirely independent of the Indian Government, and under the immediate jurisdiction of the colonial administration in London; the governor of the island is a sort of absolute monarch, and pays very little heed to the deliberations of his legislative council. To this despotic form of government, which is extremely distasteful to the constitutional Englishman, are attributed most of the defects attendant upon the administration of the beautiful island. One of the greatest of these is that the governor's term of office (four years) is entirely too short, scarcely long enough for him to become thoroughly acquainted with his domain. With a population of two millions and a half, among whom are only three thousand Europeans, the concentration of administrative power in one hand seems to be the most advantageous form of government. At all events, upon closer examination of the matter, I came to the conclusion that here, as in most of her colonies, England, with her usual practical sense, had selected what was best, and that the government of Ceylon was conducted with more circumspection and better judgment than would be the case were the island under the jurisdiction of almost any other civilized nation.

After providing myself with more introductory letters from Galle, and purchasing the necessary articles for a longer sojourn in Belligam, I loaded my sixteen chests on a large, two-wheeled bullock cart that was to carry them inside of eight days to Galle. These bullock carts are the only means for transporting freight on the public roads in Ceylon. The largest carts will carry on their two powerful wheels a load of forty hundred weight, and are drawn by four strong humped oxen or zebus of the largest species. The yoke is simply laid across the necks of the animals in front of the hump; the cart is covered by a barrel-shaped roof of plaited cocoa leaves that protects the freight in the body of the vehicle from the deluging rain; mats of the same material serve as curtains in front and at the back.

The load is carefully adjusted over the wheels so that the centre of gravity rests directly over the axle. The driver sits in front on the pole immediately behind the bullocks, or else he walks between them, and by incessant cries, or tugging at their tails, urges the poor beasts into a more rapid gait. Hundreds of such carts, some with two, some with four zebus, are continually seen on all the public roads. Among them may occasionally be seen the swifter little "oxen-drosky" or "bullock-bandy," a lighter two-wheeled vehicle of similar build, drawn by a pretty, swift-footed zebu.

On the 9th of December I took my departure from hospitable Whist Bungalow, accompanied by the good wishes and judicious counsels of my amiable hosts. The journey from Colombo to Galle is a favorite theme in all the descriptions of Ceylon travel. Until within a few years, all the mail steamers landed first at Galle, from whence the passengers were transported overland to Colombo; consequently their first impressions of the island's natural beauty were received while traveling along this road, which is, in truth, peculiarly rich in natural attractions. The cocoa-forest, with its endless succession of charming pictures, extends along the entire south-west coast. The road winds, now through the shadowy forest, now verges on the sands, or the rocks overhanging the sea, now pierces dense jungles, or crosses the picturesque bridges which span the numberless streams of the west coast. Formerly the entire journey from Colombo to Galle was made in wagons, but a railway now takes the place of the old road for about one third the distance. It also runs close to the shore, traverses the palm-grove in almost a direct line, and terminates at Caltura. The continuation of the railway from this point to Galle, which would be of incalculable advantage to the latter city, is not sanctioned by the government lest Galle's importance might outrival that of Colombo, the capital. As intercourse between the two cities is very active, and constantly increasing, the commercial success of a railway cannot be doubted. Unfortunately the disparaging wish to elevate Colombo to the detriment of Galle prompts the government to steadily refuse its concession, notwithstanding the fact that a company has proved its financial ability to complete the line. This is the cause of general complaint all along the Galle-Colombo road. The traveler is compelled either to hire a very expensive private conveyance, or to trust himself to the mail-coach, which makes daily trips between Galle and Caltura. This is also a very expensive mode of travel, and anything but agreeable.

The mail-coach bears the imposing title of "Royal mail-coach," and proudly displays on its doors the English coat-of-arms, "*Honi soit qui mal y pense!*"—an admonition which, considering the condition of the rickety vehicle, and the tortured horses furnishing the motive-power, sounds like pure irony. The coach, which is scarcely large enough to comfortably accommodate six passengers, is frequently crowded with twice that number, each of the two seats inside as well as the one behind occupied by three persons, although there is hardly room for two. The most desirable places are in front beside the driver. Here one may enjoy a view of the surrounding country, and at the same time escape the anything but agreeable odors which emanate from the perspiring, cocoa-oiled Singhalese passengers crowded inside. The fare for the five hours' journey is, for each "white" (European) passenger, fifteen rupees; the dusky native pays only half as much.

The most disagreeable feature of this coach ride, as with all similar mail-coach journeys in Ceylon, is the horrible torture inflicted on the wretched horses. The worthy Singhalese seem to be entirely ignorant of the fact that driving a horse is an art which has to be acquired, and that horses must be trained, or "adapted" to the work required of them. They seem, on the contrary, to think that the poor beasts are gifted with an intuitive or hereditary knowledge of how to draw a wagon, for, without previous training, they imprison the frightened creatures in clumsy harness, and then torture them in various ways, until in sheer desperation they gallop off. When neither urgent cries nor violent blows suffice to make them go, various devices of torture are resorted to: the sensitive nostrils are torn apart with iron hooks; the tongue is seized with a pair of tongs and almost pulled from the throat; the ears are twisted around sticks until you think they will be torn from their sockets; ropes are fastened to the fore legs, and pulled by half a dozen yelping lads, while as many more tug at the creature's tail, or beat his legs with clubs. If this is not sufficient to reduce the animal to a state of mad desperation, a lighted torch is held under his belly. In short, all the devices resorted to by the holy Inquisition to convert the unbelieving heretic are here practised on these poor dumb brutes. Often, when compelled to witness such atrocious cruelty, utterly powerless to prevent it, I have wondered what heinous crimes the wretched creatures were expiating. Who can tell but what kindred impressions pervaded the crania of our dusky coachman and groom? They doubtless are firm believers in Siva and the transmigration of souls, and imagined that by torturing the mail-coach horses, they avenged the cruelties practised on their ancestors by heartless princes and conquerors. Either this or a total want of sympathy—perhaps too he shares the peculiar belief entertained by many Europeans that animals have no feeling—actuates the Singhalese, who considers the torture of dumb beasts an amusement. In the villages along the road, where the horses are changed, the arrival of the mail-coach is the most important event of the day, and all the inhabitants assemble, partly to inspect and criticise the passengers, partly to enjoy the exciting spectacle of changing horses, and to take active part in torturing the freshly-harnessed beasts. When these are rendered desperate, they dash forward in a mad gallop that is kept up until failing breath reduces them to a more moderate pace. Covered with sweat, with foaming lips and quivering limbs, they arrive at the next station, where they are relieved for a time by their companions in misery. For the traveler who trusts himself to the rickety coach, this mode of travel is neither pleasant nor free from danger. The coach is frequently overturned and broken; sometimes the horses take it into their heads to dash across the fields, or back into banana thickets and ditches, for which reason I was prepared at any moment to leap from my elevated seat beside the driver. It is difficult to understand why the English Government, usually so rigid in maintaining order and discipline, has not long ago prohibited such cruelty to animals, and established rules for protecting the poor horses of her own "Royal mail-coach."

Great Buddha, thou that didst seek to mitigate all suffering, what a blunder hast thou committed! What a benefit to man and beast would it have been hadst thou, instead of foolishly interdicting the taking of life, forbidden torture!

While the former command is strictly obeyed by the worshipper of Buddha, he never fails to rejoice when the naturalist shoots the apes and flying foxes that steal his bananas and mangoes; or when the planter kills the elephant that tramples down his rice fields, the leopard that destroys his goats, and the marten that robs his chicken-yard. As a rule the Singhalese repulse the idea of taking life, and are very careful not to kill an animal outright. For this reason most of the fishermen are Roman Catholics; they have renounced the faith of Buddha in order that they may pursue their calling, which involves the killing of fish.

The stubborn insubordination shown by the Indian horses towards their torturers, and their inclination to make unexpected leaps from the road, requires considerable dexterity on the part of the coachman. His assistant likewise must be constantly on his guard. The perseverance and agility of the latter is really wonderful. Entirely naked, with the exception of a cloth around his loins, a white turban on his head, and a post-horn around his neck, the swarthy fellow (a Tamil) will run for a long distance beside the flying coach, tugging now at the right, now at the left rein; occasionally swinging himself to the footboard when the horses are going at their greatest speed. At the approach of another wagon from the opposite direction, or at a sudden turn in the road, he quickly seizes the horses' heads and forces them to the proper side. In crossing the long wooden bridges that span the wider streams, he checks the wild career of his steeds, and cautiously leads them over the loose, rattling planks. If a child—as frequently happens—runs into the road, or an old woman obstinately disputes the right of way with the coach, they are unceremoniously pushed aside by the Tamil groom. In short, he is constantly on the alert, ready for any emergency. Although the character of the landscape along the entire stretch of seventy miles between Colombo and Galle is the same, yet the enchanted eye of the traveler never wearies. The never-ending charm of the cocoa-groves, the inexhaustible variety of palm-groups, with their alternating pictures of human and animal life, prevent his interest from flagging. The piercing heat of the tropical sun rarely becomes oppressive, owing to the shade of the groves among which he rides and the cool breeze from the ocean. True, the feathery foliage of the palms does not cast the dense refreshing shade of our northern woods, for the sun's rays easily penetrate the plumed crowns; but luxuriant vines of all sorts entwine the slender stems, and hang in festoons from tree to tree, or swing like graceful chandeliers from their branches.

Many of the climbers are adorned with masses of exquisite bloom, such as flaming lilies, azure-hued thunbergias, rose-colored bougainvilleas, and the gorgeous butterfly blossoms of various papilionaceous creepers. Among the palms—which of course predominate—are numerous other trees, the noble mango, and the lofty bread-fruit with its ponderous crown of dark green leaves. The slim column of the graceful papaya (*Carica papaya*) is beautifully veined, and crowned by a diadem of spreading palmate leaves. Different varieties of jasmine, orange, and lemon shrubs are literally covered with fragrant white blossoms. Among them nestle the picturesque white or brown huts, and the traveler might easily imagine himself riding through a long continuous village of palm gardens, were it not for an occasional stretch of denser woods, or for the rural bazaar which, with its collection of huts, betrays the village proper.

Sometimes the road for a long distance verges upon the sea-shore, where tracts of yellow yielding sand alternate with rocky hillocks; the latter are clothed with grotesque pandanus shrubs, or screw-palms. The pandanus (*Pandanus odoratissimus*) belongs to the most singular character plants of the tropics. It is closely allied to the palms, and is also called screw-palm, or, more improperly, screw-pine. The low cylindrical stem, which grows from twenty to forty feet high, is twisted, and branched like a candelabrum; at the extremity of every branch grows a thick tuft of large sword-shaped leaves similar to those of the dracæna and the yucca. Some of the leaves are a light green, others a much darker hue; they are gracefully twisted, and their spiral arrangement around the stem gives it the appearance of a perfectly regular screw. From the base of every tuft hangs a cluster of white, deliciously fragrant flowers, or a large red fruit like the anana. But the plant's most remarkable feature is the slender adventitious roots, which give it the appearance of walking on stilts. A clump of pandanus trees offers a fantastic sight as the stems rise on their stilts above the lower shrubbery, or stalk about over the rocks along the shore.

The white or yellow sand of the beach, which is diversified by numerous dark, rocky projections, is animated by multitudes of nimble little sand crabs, whose fleetness has won for them the classic title of *Ocypode*. Also numerous hermit-crabs (*Pagurus*) deliberately wander among their swift-footed cousins, dragging after them the snail-houses in which they have hidden their soft, sensitive hinder-parts. Here and there are sand-pipers, herons, plovers, and other shore birds busily engaged in catching fish in successful competition with the Singhalese fishermen. The latter pursue their calling in groups or singly; if in companies, they row out in several canoes, and together drag a large net towards the shore. The solitary fisherman prefers to snatch his prey from the yeasty surf, and an interesting spectacle is afforded by the naked brown forms, protected only by broad-brimmed straw hats, dashing fearlessly with their hand-nets into the foaming breakers. The refreshing bath seems to delight them as much as it does their offspring, who play in swarms along the beach, and, at the age of six or eight, are masters of the noble art of swimming.

Like a binding of lovely satin ribbon the white or golden sands stretch for miles along the deeply dented coast, separating the deep blue of the ocean from the pale green of the cocoa-forest. The beauty of the shore is enhanced by the slender palms that incline their feathered crests towards the water as if eager to drink in deep draughts of the invigorating breeze and radiant sunshine. The ground at their feet is profusely decorated with the most beautiful strand-flowers, among which three species are particularly noticeable: the goat's-foot (*Ipomea pes capri*), with its wealth of crimson blossoms; an exquisite rose-colored balsam (*Impatiens*), and the imposing trumpet-lily (*Pancratium ceylonicum*); the stately white flowers of the latter, with their narrow overhanging petals, grow in clusters on a slender stem six or eight feet high. The huge leaves of the calla also furnish adornment for the wayside. When the rays of the sun become intolerable, or a sudden shower overtakes him, the Singhalese merely plucks a giant caladium leaf that protects him more effectively than would a cotton or silk umbrella, and is, with its delicate traceries, certainly more ornamental. Thus, in this sunlit Eden, even parasols may be had for the plucking, or, better still, "*entout cas*," for the caladium leaf answers the double purpose of umbrella and sunshade.

Among the many attractions of this beautiful Galle-Colombo road, are the numerous deltas which interrupt the cocoa-forest, and the extensive lagoons that connect the rivers, especially of the northern part of the coast (between Colombo and Caltura). The former sovereigns of the island, the Dutch, were so delighted with these natural water-ways, which reminded them of their native country, that they established a regular system of canals, and entirely neglected the roads by land. Like the well-known "Treckschuiten" of the Netherlands, numerous freight-boats then plied the waters of the coast lagoons, and transacted the greater part of the commercial business. Since the construction of excellent roads by the English, these lagoons are rarely used. However, with the dense groves of bamboo and palm fringing their banks, with the charming little islands and rock-groups dotting their mirror-like surface, they offer to the traveler hastening by a wealth of enchanting pictures, especially there, where, above the dark green forest mass, are arrayed hosts of slender cocoa-palms—as Humboldt aptly expresses it, "a forest above the forest." A fitting background is formed by the ranges of blue hills in the distance; here and there loom the taller summits of the highland mountains, among them the ever present, ever conspicuous Peak of Adam.

The smiling landscape assumes a more serious aspect where the larger streams debouch on the sea. Here, the sombre mangrove is the most salient feature. The shore is densely fringed with these trees, their overarching roots forming impenetrable thickets which were formerly inhabited by crocodiles, but the steady march of civilization has driven them to the upper portions of the rivers. The largest of these rivers is the Kalu-ganga (black river), which, for miles from its mouth, is as wide as the Rhine at Cologne. Caltura, the terminus of the railway, is situated at its mouth. At the southern extremity of Caltura a magnificent banyan tree spans the road like a triumphal arch. This gigantic fig-tree has sent out its powerful air-roots, which have taken root in the opposite side of the road, thus forming, with the parent stem, a natural arch that is all the more attractive from its parasitic adornments—ferns, orchids, and creepers of all sorts, that twine among the branches with wanton luxuriance.

During a later visit to Caltura, I discovered near the shore a second plant-wonder; it was an ancient India-rubber tree whose reticulated roots formed a veritable labyrinth in which swarms of merry children romped and played at hide and seek.

Another attractive point of the Galle-Colombo road is the rest-house at Bentotte, at which the passengers of the "Royal mail-coach" are allowed to rest, and refresh themselves with breakfast. A peculiar delicacy served at this meal are the celebrated oysters of Bentotte, which may be had raw, broiled, or pickled. From the rest-house, which is picturesquely situated between lofty tamarind trees on a hill, there is a fine view of the ocean, and the bridge which spans the river. After breakfast I rambled down to the bridge, below which some natives were dredging for oysters, then through the picturesque bazaars of the long village street. The traffic in these bazaars is in as perfect accord with their idyllic surroundings as are the unpretending huts, and the primitive costumes of their half naked inhabitants. Among the most important articles of commerce, rice and curry form the most necessary food, betel and areca the favorite luxury. These, together with other articles of trade, are tastefully spread out on fresh banana leaves in the open shops, whose sole entrance answers the double purpose of door and windows. Alternating with heaps of cocoa-nuts are luscious bananas, nutritious yams, colocasia, etc. Among them are gigantic bread-fruits, weighing from fifty to eighty pounds, the closely allied jack fruit, delicate mangoes and annonas (the custard-apple of the English). While the fragrance of the noble fruits exposed for sale in these shops, which are tastefully decorated by their Singhalese proprietors, is pleasant and agreeable, intense odors, which are anything but delightful, occasionally assail our olfactories; they emanate from the heaps of dried sea animals, principally fish and crabs; of the latter, particularly large shrimps—here called prawns—are favorite ingredients for the omnipresent "rice and curry."

Disappointment awaits the traveler who expects to find in these Ceylonese bazaars the noise and confusion which characterize the markets of most peoples, especially those of southern Europe. Who, for instance, that is familiar with the stir and bustle of the Piazza dell' Erbe in Verona, or the turmoil of Santa Lucia in Naples, would not expect to find far more confusion in a tropical bazaar? Such is not the case. The sedate, placid temperament of the Singhalese is evident in his commercial relations, when the interest of both buyer and seller is as trifling as the coin with which he buys the most luscious fruits. These coins, by the way, are copper pieces, of one and five cents value. One hundred of the former, twenty of the latter make a rupee; their impress is a cocoa-palm. Although the Singhalese is not wholly indifferent to money, he seems to require it less than most of mother earth's children, for the reason that few of her regions are so lavishly supplied with nature's noblest gifts as this fortunate island. As much rice as he requires to sustain life may be procured at the expense of very little labor; from ten to fifteen cents will supply all his daily wants, while the fruits of the earth, and the fishes of the sea are so abundant that components for a curry, and various other mixtures, are never lacking.

Then why should the Singhalese embitter his life with toil? He is too indolent, or, rather, too philosophical. For this reason we see him stretched at his ease in front of his primitive habitation, or squatted on the ground lazily gossiping with his neighbors. The trifling work his garden requires is soon performed, and the remaining time passed in play. Even his amusements are anything but exciting; the magic spell of rest and quiet seems to have settled on these fortunate beings—a condition that is as strange as delightful to the restless culture-folk of the nineteenth century.

Fortunate Singhalese! No care for the morrow or the more distant future troubles you. What you require for the nourishment of yourself and your children grows spontaneously into your very mouth; your luxuries are obtained by the most trifling exertion. You are indeed like the "lilies of the field," that wanton around your simple dwelling; you "toil not, neither do you spin," yet are you nourished by a providential nature! No political or warlike ambition tortures your soul; no disturbing thought of competition, or rise and fall of stocks, drives slumber from your eyes! Those aspirations of higher culture: titles, orders, are unknown to you, and yet you rejoice in your life! I am almost tempted to believe you do not envy the European's thousand-and-one superfluous needs; you are content to remain nature's children—content with your paradisal existence. How comfortably you lie there, dreamily watching the dancing sunlight among the feathery plumes of your cocoa canopy; how you enjoy your betel, your children's games, your refreshing bath in the river; how easily you accomplish your simple toilet! What careburdened civilian would not covet your innocent nature and your paradisal rest?

These and kindred reflections passed through my brain while the coach was changing horses at the last station before Galle, where groups of indolent natives were enjoying life in the shade of the bananas. Here, indeed, the "struggle for existence" seemed to have ceased! I was roused from my reverie by the two horse-tamers who asked me to resume my place on the front seat, the noble Malabars at the same moment suggesting in broken English, that it was time to think of the customary "fee" to the coachman and groom, as after the arrival at Galle they would be too busy to properly attend to this momentous transaction. I had noticed that an opulent native passenger on reaching his destination had given each of the men a "double-anna" and believed myself sufficiently taxed as "white man" if I paid four times that amount. I handed to each a shilling, but my gratuity was indignantly rejected by both the men, who read me a joint lecture on the importance of color that was certainly very complimentary to my complexion. The purport of this homily was, that every white "gentleman" was expected to bestow at least one rupee on each of the men, and that I—who must belong to one of the highest castes, by reason of my fair complexion and light hair—would be expected to pay considerably more. Although taxation levied in this manner could not fail to tickle my vanity, I was not to be inveigled into paying more than the usual "white-tax." I gave each of the men a rupee, and had the satisfaction afterwards of hearing myself pronounced a "perfect gentleman." When I considered the exquisite enjoyment of the delightful five-hours' coach ride, I found the exorbitant fare of seventeen florins quite reasonable, and was really very sorry, notwithstanding the heat and weariness, when the light-tower of Galle came in sight. Shortly after, the mail-coach rumbled over the drawbridge of the ancient moat, through a long gloomy gateway, to the door of the "Oriental Hotel" of Galle.

IX.

PUNTO GALLA.

ON a rocky promontory that extends from the west and encloses the roomy harbor, stands lovely Punto Galla or Point de Galle, from remote antiquity one of the most celebrated and important cities of Ceylon. The definition of the Singhalese Galla is "rocks," and bears no relation whatever to the Latin *gallus*, as the island's first European masters, the Portuguese, supposed. An illustration of this erroneous interpretation remains to this day on the ancient city wall, in the moss-grown stone image of a cock with the numerals 1640.

Galle, according to the testimony of ancient authors, was an important commercial emporium, and probably the largest and wealthiest city on the island more than two thousand years ago. Here, the eastern and western halves of the old world met and clasped hands; here, the Arabian navigator who ventured thus far from his Persian Gulf, traded with the Malay from the Sunda Archipelago, and with the Chinese from the remote East. The Oriental Tarshish of the ancient Phoenician and Hebrew writers must have been Galle; the apes and peacocks, the ivory and the gold which the navigators of those days brought from far-famed Tarshish, were designated by the same terms that are applied to them to-day by the Tamils of Ceylon; while the more accurate descriptions of the oft-visited harbor of Tarshish can be applied to but one of all Ceylon's harbors —to the celebrated "rocky point," Punto Galla.

Galle's natural advantages and geographical position near the southernmost point of Ceylon—under the sixth degree of latitude—as well as her climatic and topographical conditions, are so obvious that one would naturally suppose them all-sufficient to establish her precedence as the most important commercial station on the coast. But the continual efforts of the British Government to elevate Colombo at the expense of Galle, and especially the improved facilities of communication between Colombo and the interior of the island, as well as her nearer proximity to the coffee districts, have in late years considerably injured Galle. As I remarked before, by far the largest portion of the island's trade has withdrawn to Colombo, and Galle's beautiful harbor is not what it once was. However, Galle still remains the most important seaboard town *next* to Colombo, and especially will she continue to be the natural outlet for the rich products of the south province. Chief among these are the manifold properties of the cocoa-palm: the superior cocoa oil; coir, the stout fibres of the cocoanut which is used principally for the manufacture of cordage; palm sugar, from which arrack is distilled, etc. Formerly Galle played an important part in the gem traffic, which she still does in the graphite or plumbago trade. If the railway were to be completed from Caltura to Galle, and the rocks and coral-reefs which render parts of the excellent harbor dangerous, were removed with dynamite, then would Punto Galla's vanished prosperity be restored and flourish with renewed vigor.

The situation of Galle is charming, and it is quite natural that in nearly all the earlier descriptions of Ceylon travel this point, on which the voyager first debarked, should be specially mentioned and extolled. The European or "white town"—the "fort"—occupies the crest of the rocky tongue of land before mentioned, and consists of one-storied stone houses, encircled by wide verandas which are upheld by rows of pillars, and covered by projecting tile roofs. Flourishing gardens add as much to the adornment of the city as the broad avenues of shade-dispensing suriya (*Thespesia populnea*) and hibiscus trees (*Hibiscus rosa sinensis*). The latter here take the place of the rose tree; they are covered with crisp, shining green foliage and lovely crimson flowers, which the English resident prosaically designates "shoe-flowers," because a decoction of their fruit is used to polish shoes.

The most conspicuous among the public buildings is the Protestant church, a handsome Gothic structure built on one of the highest points of the hilly city. Its thick stone walls and garland of shade trees render the vaulted interior delightfully cool, it was decidedly refreshing when, one Sunday forenoon, tired by an extended ramble, I sought shelter from the too ardent rays of Helios in this shadowy retreat.

Opposite the church is the "Queen's House," the largest edifice in Galle, and formerly the official residence of the governor. Here, travelers of rank, or those furnished with special commendations, were hospitably entertained by the governor; and this, perhaps, is why the government building in Galle and its near neighborhood, are usually the first points mentioned and admired in the earlier descriptions of Ceylon travel. Among the German travelers who have been entertained here are Messrs. Hoffmeister and Ransonnet. Several years ago this "house of the Queen" passed into private hands, and is now the property of Messrs. Clark, Spence & Co., the largest mercantile house in the city. I brought letters of introduction from Herr Stipperger to the head of this firm, Mr. Henry Scott, by whom I was most cordially received. Two of the elegant, roomy apartments in the "Queen's House" and a breezy veranda were placed at my disposal, and everything done to render my sojourn in Galle as pleasant as possible.

I not only felt at home in Mr. Scott's agreeable family circle, but learned to know in him an English merchant whose varied attainments eminently fit him for the prominent positions he occupies.

At present he represents several European consulates, and it is to be regretted that he was not also chosen to be Germany's consular representative. The present incumbent of that office in Galle, Mr. Vanderspaar, does not speak German, nor does he exhibit the least interest for the country he represents. Judging from the reports of former travelers I infer that Mr. Vanderspaar's father and predecessor in office was distinguished by the same negative qualities. On the other hand, Mr. Scott, who spent a number of years at school in Germany, speaks the language of that country with great fluency, and entertains a high regard for German literature and science. Having the good fortune to be considered a representative of the latter I enjoyed every advantage Mr. Scott's liberal hospitality could supply. Such treatment naturally reduced me to a state of indecision, whether it would not be wiser to accept his generous offer and set up my zoological laboratory for several weeks among the European comforts and conveniences of the "Queen's House," and in the midst of a pleasant family circle, than in Belligam surrounded by semi-savages.

However, I manfully resisted the allurements of the former alternative, and was richly rewarded for it; in Belligam I obtained a better view of the primitive nature of Ceylon and its aboriginal inhabitants than I could have in civilized Galle.

The short time I remained in the latter city, as well as the brief visit I paid Mr. Scott on my return from Belligam, was, by the circumspect aid of that gentleman, so profitably spent that, notwithstanding the brevity of the period, I obtained an excellent insight into the natural beauties around Galle, and the wealth of her magnificent coral banks. At any hour I might elect, both of Mr. Scott's carriages were at my disposal for an excursion by land, and his comfortable boat—manned by three stout Malabars—at my command for an expedition by water. Besides, Mr. Scott introduced me to several prominent English residents who could materially assist me in my scientific investigations; to Captains Bayley and Blythe in particular I am greatly indebted for numerous favors.

The first and most convenient promenade after arriving in Galle is usually a tour around the fort on the high walls. These walls, which were solidly built of brick by the Dutch, rise to a considerable elevation above the water; from the east wall may be obtained a fine view of the harbor, the wooded hills encircling it, and the blue mountain chains of the distant highlands. From the south and west walls one looks down on the wonderful coral banks that girt the rocky promontory on every side. These coral gardens which, at ebb tide, display a large portion of their flower-like animals, are especially beautiful near the light-tower at the south-west corner of the fort. Two ancient gateways whose stone pillars, like the walls, are covered with luxuriant ferns and mosses, lead from the interior of the fort into the open. The east gate opens on the quay; the one on the north side opens on the esplanade, a green level stretch that separates the fort from the *pettah*, or "Black Town." The latter comprises the simple habitations and bazaars of the natives; part of it extends in an easterly direction along the mole around the harbor, another section stretches along the shore and the Colombo road. Both lose themselves without definite limits among the groups of houses and clusters of huts that are scattered everywhere in the surrounding cocoa-groves.

In a beautiful situation on a neighboring hill opposite the fort, is the Catholic church, with which are connected a Catholic school and mission. In the director of the latter, Padre Palla (the successor of the esteemed Padre Miliani—frequently mentioned in former books of travel), I found a very agreeable and well-informed gentleman; he is a native of Triest, and was greatly delighted to find me able to converse with him about that city and Dalmatia in his beloved Italian mother tongue. The well-kept mission garden is, like most of the gardens in the Eden-like environs of Galle, rich in the magnificent productions of the tropical zone- wonders that would delight the heart of every botanist and plant friend.

But the most enchanting spot, to my taste, in the whole neighborhood is Captain Bayley's "Villa Marina." This enterprising gentleman was formerly a ship captain, and is now the agent for the P. and O. Company. His intense love for nature prompted him to select for his residence a spot that for wild and picturesque beauty cannot be surpassed. About midway in the wide semicircular sweep of shore which encloses the northern part of the harbor, two huge masses of gneiss rock jut far out into the ocean; several small rock islets, densely overgrown with pandanus shrubs, are grouped like sentinels around them. On one of these rock masses (the one farthest towards the east) Captain Bayley has built a tasteful villa that, with its lovely garden, forms a veritable "Miramare of Galla." From the west windows of the villa, and particularly from the terrace outside, one enjoys a view of the city and the intervening harbor that is not surpassed by any point of view in the neighborhood. The light-tower and the Protestant church are salient features in the beautiful panorama, and are especially attractive when illumined by the golden radiance of the morning sun. A charming middle ground is offered by the picturesque black rock-islets with their fantastic decorations of screw-palms; and the little Singhalese fishing huts nestling at their feet. For the foreground, the cloven rocks tossed about, and heaped up in the wildest disorder in the immediate vicinity of the villa, will furnish a grotesque motive—or, if a friendlier character is desired for the picture, then copy a stretch of the lovely garden with its adornments of choicest tropical plants.

Among the numerous embellishments of this garden are several splendid examples of the Egyptian dhum-palm (*Hyphæne thebaica*), in which I was specially interested. The strong stem of this palm is not, like most of the trees belonging to this family, a slender column, but is repeatedly forked like the dragon-tree, or *dracæna;* every branch bears a crown of fan-shaped leaves. I had made the acquaintance of this celebrated palm—which grows principally in Upper Egypt—in the Arabian village of Tur, at the foot of Mt. Sinai, and have given an illustration of it in my *Arabischen Korallen* (plate iv. p. 28). You may, therefore, imagine how surprised I was when I here beheld the same tree in so different a guise that I scarcely recognized it. The adapting it to the totally different conditions of life in Ceylon had transformed the Egyptian dhum-palm to quite another tree. The powerful stem seemed at least twice as strong and far more vigorous than in its native land; the forked branches were more numerous, but shorter and more compact; the gigantic fan-shaped leaves much larger, more luxuriant, and more succulent; the flowers and fruit seemed also to have increased in size and beauty. Indeed the entire *habitus* of the beautiful tree had so changed in the forcing-house climate of Ceylon that the most essential features of its inherited physiognomy seemed to have entirely disappeared. And all this had been accomplished by the changed conditions—above all, the increased humidity of the atmosphere—of this tree, accustomed from its earliest infancy to the hot, dry climate of the North African deserts. The stately dhum-palms in the Villa Marina garden were grown from seed brought from Egypt, and in the space of twenty years have attained a height of thirty feet!

A large portion of the villa is taken up by an extensive fernery. Ferns thrive excellently well in the natural forcing-house climate of Ceylon, and Captain Bayley, in addition to a choice selection of the most beautiful native ferns, has a number of remarkable exotics. Here one may at a glance view the entire wealth of delicate and attractive forms which are unfolded by these exquisite cryptograms. Nor is there a lack of tree ferns, selaginellas and lycopodiæ.

There are charms for the zoologist as well as for the botanist in this miramare of Galla. A miniature menagerie in the lower court contains a number of curious mammals and birds, besides an ostrich from New Holland, several owls and parrots, and a native ant-eater (*Manis*). The latter, together with several curious fish, Captain Bayley was kind enough to present to me; and on Christmas, after I had gone to Belligam, he sent me another interesting gift in the shape of a pair of loris (*Stenops*). But far more attractive to me than these curious animals were the exquisite corals that literally cover the rocks surrounding Villa Marina; even the little harbor in which Captain Bayley moors his boats, and the stone piers of the landing-place are thickly coated with these lovely creatures. A great many other marine animals that inhabit the Galle coral banks are also to be found crowded into this limited space: huge black sea-urchins and red sea-stars, multitudes of crabs and fish, beautifully variegated snails and mussels, curious worms of different classes, and whatever the motley company may be called that lives, moves, and has its being among the branches of the coral trees. For this reason Captain Bayley's villa, which he is willing to dispose of on account of his removal to Colombo, is peculiarly adapted for a zoological station, and is besides but half a mile from the city.

If you ramble along the rocky shore in an easterly direction around the bay of Galle, you will gradually ascend one of the higher outlooks from which there is another beautiful view of the city and harbor, and which is fitly named "Bella Vista." Here a Protestant clergyman, the Rev. Mr. Marx, has built himself a handsome villa and established a mission.

The thickly-wooded hill, which juts into the water in a southerly direction, ends abruptly in a steep rocky bluff that faces the light-tower on the opposite shore of the harbor. There was a project at one time to fortify this point, but it was never carried into effect. Several cannon still peer from the tangled masses of wanton creepers; a merry company of apes were frolicking over the bluff the Sunday afternoon I visited it. The narrow path I followed for some distance led me along the steep rocky shore into a dense thicket of pandanus trees and lianas. The thicket is cloven by a deep ravine, along the bottom of which a mountain brook leaps merrily towards the sea. Near its mouth the stream falls into a natural basin of rock, and this is a favorite bathing resort for the native inhabitants of Galle. The day I came unexpectedly from the thicket I surprised a dusky group of bathers, of both sexes, disporting themselves in the cool water of the "Onawatty Basin."

There is another similar rock basin below the bluff; it is called the "watering place," because its abundant flow supplies most of the ships with delicious drinking water. The walls of rock which enclose this natural basin are overgrown with thorny date-palms (*Phœnix sylvestris*), snowy-blossomed asclepias, and green-gray euphorbias (*Euphorbia antiquorum*), that resemble a huge "girandole cactus;" they, together with their "wooden-legged" neighbors, the pandanus trees, belong to the most peculiar growths of these thickets.

Quite a different character from the savage rocks on the south-east of Galle, is shown by the placid valleys extending between the rows of wooded hills north of the city. Here the idyllic character of the south-west coast again predominates. A favorite excursion in this direction is to "Wackwelle Hill," on whose summit an excellent carriage road winds through a beautiful grove of cocoa-palms. In the grove, which is a favorite resort for picnic parties from the city, an enterprising speculator lately opened a restaurant, and charges every visitor, whether he patronizes the establishment or not, a sixpence for the lovely view. The latter comprises the broad, verdure-clad valley of the Gindura River, which empties into the sea half a mile north of the city. Like a glittering ribbon of silver the river winds among the crisp green rice fields, the "paddy fields" that cover the lower portions of the valley. The slopes on either side are adorned with the most luxuriant shrubbery that is animated everywhere by multitudes of apes and parrots. In the distance rise the ever-present mountain ranges of the highlands, and towering above them, the stately "Haycock," which takes its name from its peculiar form, a bell-shaped stack of hay. This peak is visible for a long distance, and serves as a landmark for approaching ships.

But more enchanting than the land gardens in the vicinity of Galle are the submarine gardens of coral that encircle the walls of the fort, and I still regret that I was not able to devote weeks instead of a few days to their investigation. In this particular Ransonnet, the Vienna artist, was more fortunate. Aided by the best of modern appliances for marine investigations—among them an improved diving-bell—he devoted several weeks to studying the coral banks in Galle harbor, and has given an excellent description of them in his illustrated work on Ceylon. (Westermann, Brunswick, 1868.) Four colored plates, for which he made the sketches under water in his diving-bell, illustrate animal life in this mysterious coral world.

Nine years ago, when I visited the coral banks of the Red Sea at Tur, on the Sinai coast, and for the first time saw the wonderful formation of these enchanted submarine gardens, my highest interest was excited, and I attempted in my popular lectures on "Arabian Corals" (Berlin, 1876) to briefly describe the organization of the remarkable animals, and their connection with various other creatures. The corals of Ceylon, with which I became acquainted in Galle and Belligam, vividly recalled those delightful experiences, and enriched me with an abundance of new ones.

The Indian marine fauna of Ceylon is closely allied to the Arabian fauna of the Red Sea, both having many genera and species in common. But the number and variety of different organisms is considerably larger in the broad basin of the Indian Ocean, with its diversified coast development, than in the circumscribed limits of the

Arabian Gulf, with its uniform and monotonous conditions of life. I also found that, in spite of the apparent similarity of the coral banks in these two regions, there was considerable difference between their general physiognomy. While the predominant hues of those at Tur are a warm yellow, red, orange, and brown; the prevailing color in the coral gardens of Ceylon is green—green in all its various shades and tones. Yellow-green Alcyonia stand beside sea-green Heteropora; malachite-green Anthophylla beside olive-green Millepora; emerald-green Madrepora and Astreæ beside brown-green Montipora and Meandrina.

Ransonnet justly remarked the striking predominance of green everywhere in Ceylon. Not only is the greater part of this "ever-green isle" ornamented the whole year through with an unfading carpet of verdure, but a majority of the animals that inhabit it are conspicuously green. The most numerous birds and lizards, butterflies and beetles are decked in brilliant green, as are also many of the marine creatures of widely different classes, namely, fish and crabs, worms (*Amphinomæ*) and sea-roses (*Actinia*); why, even animals that elsewhere seldom or never don the green livery, here wear it as a constant uniform, as, for instance, several members of the star-fish family (*Ophiura*), sea-urchins, sea-cucumbers, giant mussels (*Tridacna*), spirula and others of a similar character. An explanation of this phenomenon may be deduced from the Darwinian theory of selection, especially from the law of adaptation as applied to the "sympathetic selection of color," which I have demonstrated in my *Natural History of the Creation* (seventh ed., p. 235). The less the predominant color of an animal differs from that of its environments, the less likely is it to attract the notice of its foes, the easier it can unobserved approach its prey, and consequently, the more it is likely to be favored in the "struggle for existence." Natural selection, therefore, constantly increases the harmony between the prevailing hue of the organism and that of its environments, because it is of advantage to the former. The coral banks of Ceylon, with their predominant green inhabitants, as aptly illustrate this theory as the green land animals that animate the ever-verdant thickets of the island. But the former surpass the latter in purity and brilliancy of coloring.

It would be a mistake to conclude that this excess of a single color would become monotonous. On the contrary one never wearies of its various tones and exquisite modifications. Besides it enhances the beauty of various other hues; the lovely red, yellow, violet, and blue tints of many birds and insects are rendered doubly attractive by reason of their contrast with the dark green forests of Ceylon. So with the same brilliant hues of many of the sea animals on the coral banks. Especially conspicuous for their splendid coloring and peculiar markings, are many of the small fishes and crabs that seek nourishment among the branches of the coral trees. Some of the corals are also highly colored; for instance, many *Procilloporæ* are rose-colored, many star-corals are red or yellow, many Heteroporæ and Madreporæ are violet and brown, etc. Unfortunately these exquisite tints are for the most part extremely transitory, and vanish directly the corals are taken from the water, and frequently on being merely touched. The sensitive animals, those with widely extended cilia, and magnificent with brilliant coloring, then suddenly contract, and become dull, colorless, and shapeless.

If the gorgeous hues of the coral gardens and their motley inhabitants charm the eye, then will it be completely fascinated with the beauty and variety of form unfolded by these diminutive creatures. As each one of the radiant coral individuals may fitly be compared to a lovely flower, so the united groups may be said to resemble trees and shrubs. Formerly, indeed, corals were universally believed to be actual plants, and it was a long time before the world became convinced of their true animal nature.

At ebb tide, when the water is perfectly calm, the coral gardens offer an enchanting and fairy-like spectacle. Near the fort the water is so shallow that the keel of the boat grates upon the callous animal groups, and so clear that you can plainly distinguish the coral trees from the top of the walls. Such an abundance of beautiful and remarkable forms are concentrated in this narrow space that I was able in a few days to make a splendid collection.

Mr. Scott's garden, in which he kindly allowed me to dry my collection, presented a very curious appearance. The magnificent tropical plants seemed to vie with the strange usurpers from the sea for the prize of beauty and brilliancy of coloring, while the happy naturalist, intoxicated with delight, rambled among them, unable to decide whether the prize should be given to the flora or the fauna. The corals with all their exquisite varieties of form imitated the most beautiful plant forms, while the orchids and spice-lilies in turn simulated insects. The two great kingdoms of the organic world here seemed to have made an exchange of form.

The majority of the corals I collected in Galle, and later in Belligam, were obtained with the assistance of divers. These I found as skilful and persevering as the Arabian divers at Tur. Armed with strong iron chisels they would loosen large blocks of the calcareous structures and carefully raise them to the surface of the water. Many of the blocks weighed from fifty to eighty pounds, and required no little dexterity and labor to be safely deposited in the boat. Some corals are so brittle they break with their own weight when lifted from the water. It is, therefore, unfortunately impossible to secure unbroken specimens of many of the most attractive forms. Among the most brittle corals are certain delicate *Turbinariæ* whose convoluted stems resemble inverted cones, while some of the many-pronged *Heteroporæ*, are like colossal, hundred-branched stag-horns.

The entire attraction of a coral bank cannot be seen from above, even though you float immediately over it at ebb tide, and the water is so shallow your boat scrapes against the points. A descent into the fluid element is therefore necessary. Not possessing a diving-bell I attempted to swim to the bottom, keeping my eyes open, and after considerable practice accomplished this feat. Quite wonderful, then, is the mystical green glimmer that illumines the whole of this submarine world. The fascinated eye is continually surprised by the most remarkable light-effects, quite different from those of the familiar upper world with its "rosy radiance," and doubly curious and interesting are the forms and movements of all the thousand different creatures swarming in the coral gardens. The diver is in a new world. Here are multitudes of remarkable fishes, crabs, snails, mussels, star-creatures, worms, etc., whose nourishment consists exclusively of the flesh of the coral animals on which their habitations are fixed; and these coral-devourers—one may appropriately term them "parasites"—have, through adaptation to their peculiar mode of life, acquired the most astonishing forms, and have been furnished with weapons of defence and offence of the most singular shapes.

But, if the naturalist may not ramble free from danger among palms, neither may he swim unmolested among coral banks. The Oceanidæ, who jealously guard these cool fairy regions of the sea, threaten the intruder with a thousand dangers. The fire-corals (millepora), as well as the medusæ swimming among their branches, sting, when touched, like the most resentful nettles. The floating *cilia* of many of the mailed fishes (*Synanceia*) inflict wounds that are as painful and dangerous as those of a scorpion. Many crabs nip in the severest manner with their powerful claws. Black sea-urchins (*Diadema*) bore their barbed spines, a foot long, into the flesh, where they break off and cause annoying sores. But the worst damage to the venturesome diver is inflicted by the corals themselves. The thousands of sharp points on their calcareous structures cut and abrade the skin in various ways. In all my life I never had such an excoriated and lacerated body as when coral-fishing at Punto Galla, and I suffered from the wounds for several weeks. But what are these transitory sufferings to the naturalist whose whole life has been enriched by the marvellous experiences and natural enjoyments of his visit to the wonderful banks of coral !

X.

BELLAGEMMA.

BELLAGEMMA—beautiful gem ! How often I think of thee ! How often thy matchless image hovers before my vision and calls to mind a world of enchanting reminiscences ! Truly, if Ceylon is the diadem of India, then art thou its most transcendent jewel ! *Bella gemma della Taprobane!*

The kindly-disposed reader will, I hope, pardon me for the unwarrantable liberty I have taken with the orthography of Belligam, which means something vastly different from "beautiful gem." The original Singhalese name of the village is Weligama (which is sand-village, from *weli*, sand, and *gama*, village). But the English always speak of it as Belligam, and so we need only substitute an a for the i to give the word an Italian sound and signification which aptly describe the rare charms of the lovely spot. In my remembrance at least "Bella-gemma" will ever be connected with a gem of transcendent lustre, while the sandy beach that gave "Weligama" its name is thrust into the remote background.

After concluding to set up my zoological laboratory for several months in Belligam, I naturally sought to inform myself as to its conditions of life. In spite of repeated inquiries, however, I could learn nothing but that the village was pleasantly situated in a cocoa grove, that its sheltered harbor abounded in coral, and that the rest-house was fairly comfortable. The negative reports were: that neither European resident nor European civilization was to be found in or near Belligam—all of which I soon found to be very true. The mystic veil of adventure and strangeness enveloped my near future, and I confess that it was not without a secret misgiving and a certain sense of insecurity that I bade adieu, on the 12th of December, to Galle and European culture.

In Colombo and Kandy I had seen how near to aboriginal nature obtruded the culture-varnish of Europe, and how narrow was the dividing line between primitive forest and densely-populated city. In the most southerly portions of the island I might expect to find these conditions exaggerated; consequently all my hopes and expectations were centred on the official document I had received from the governor, and on the tried good fortune which had never yet deserted me.

Thus, full of expectation, I took my seat in the light wagon which was to convey me along the south coast to Belligam. It was five o'clock in the morning, and still quite dark, when I drove out from the fort and through the *pettah* along the harbor in a southerly direction. Softly slumbering lay the Singhalese wrapped in white cotton sheets on the palm mats in front of their silent huts. Not a sound was to be heard. The deepest silence and solitude lingered over the peaceful landscape. All this was suddenly changed by the magic wand of the rising sun, whose first gleams roused life and motion among the somnolent palms. Several birds lifted up their voices in the tops of the trees; the frolicsome palm squirrel quitted his nest and began his morning promenade up and down the cocoa stems, and the indolent "cabragoya," the huge green lizard (*Hydrosaurus*) stretched his lazy limbs on the verge of the pools. In the gardens beyond the limits of the city, nimble apes sported among the fruit trees from which they had just stolen their breakfast.

Soon the natives began to stir, and whole families assembled to enjoy their morning bath along the public highway.

Among the many novel impressions which astonish the European traveler in the equatorial regions, is the absence of twilight—that dreamy transition period between day and darkness which plays so important a part in our northern romance and poetry. Scarcely has the radiant sun, that but a moment before gilded the entire landscape with effulgent glory, vanished into the blue waters of the ocean, when swarthy night spreads her downy pinions over land and sea; and broad daylight as quickly succeeds the dusk of early morning. Here Aurora, the rosy-fingered goddess of the dawn, has lost her sway. But all the more brilliant is the young day for his unheralded approach, while the sunlight, broken into a thousand rays by the feathery palm leaves, is all the brighter for its sudden coming. The dewdrops hang like diamonds from every leaf point, and the glossy plumes of the bananas glitter in the sunshine like a thousand mirrors. The gentle morning breeze from the sea gives motion to the lovely plant forms, as well as refreshing coolness to the traveler. Everything breathes with new, fresh life and enjoyment.

The same features characterize the fifteen miles of excellent road between Galle and Belligam that were described between the former place and Colombo. Only here the cocoa-groves seem even more luxuriant, more abundant, if possible, than farther north. Multitudes of climbing plants festoon the palms with exquisite garlands of verdure and bloom, while the banana groups, papayas, and breadfruit trees encircling the lowly huts, the dainty manihots and yams in the hedges, the giant caladium and colocasia alongside the road, all seem more flourishing, more vigorous than nearer Colombo. Besides, the cocoa-groves are enlivened by numerous little ponds decked with lotus blossoms and other aquatic plants, and traversed by roistering brooks whose banks are fringed with the loveliest ferns.

Then come more rocky hillocks covered with fragrant pandanus shrubs, alternating stretches of sand carpeted with crimson convolvuli, white lilies, and other showy flowers. At the mouths of the small coast streams which intersect our road appear the stately bamboos and sombre mangroves; among them the curious stemless napa-palm with its feathered crest just lifted above the water.

Thus the eye never wearies of the beautiful plant forms, and I was almost sorry when, after a rapid drive of several hours, my Tamil coachman pointed towards a distant promontory that jutted far out into the sea and said:

"Weligama on the other side."

Soon the detached huts along the road became more numerous, and grouped themselves into village streets; on either side were crisp green rice fields interspersed with lovely groves. The stones in the walls are chiefly blocks of coral. A sudden turn brought us in sight of an eminence to the left of the road, on which stands an imposing Buddha temple, called *Agrabuddha-Ganni*, a famous resort for devout pilgrims. Close by, to the right of the road, and shaded by a kitool palm, is a colossal statue (carved in relief from the black rock) of one of the ancient kings, "Kustia Raja." His powerful frame is covered with scale-armor, and crowned by a mitre. The ancient chronicles not only extol his prowess as a conqueror, but laud him as the benefactor of Ceylon for teaching the Singhalese the use of the cocoanut. Soon after passing this statue we drove through a little bazaar, and in a few minutes more halted in front of the long-dreamed-of rest-house of Belligam.

Around the gate of the wall which encloses the rest-house garden was a dense throng of inquisitive human beings, among whom I noticed several distinguished natives of the highest caste. In pursuance of the governor's command, the president of the south province (or government agent, which is his less imposing title) had informed the head-men of Belligam of my intended visit, and had also directed them to welcome me with becoming respect.

The first head-man, or "mudlyar," a stately man of perhaps sixty years, with a good-natured countenance and a flourishing beard, approached the wagon and greeted me with a ceremonious speech in broken English. He assured me, with extreme politeness and dignity, that his whole "korle" or village felt highly honored by my visit, and that its four thousand dusky inhabitants would endeavor to make my stay among them as pleasant as possible. As for himself, he was at my command whenever I chose to call upon his services. A vigorous drumming, accomplished by several energetic tom-tom beaters in the background, on the conclusion of this formal reception-speech, corroborated its official importance.

After I had answered and thanked the mudlyar, he introduced me to the important personages in his suite: the second head-man, or Arachy, the collector of taxes, and the doctor, as well as to some of the more distinguished citizens of Belligam, all of whom assured me in the friendliest manner that they were ready to assist me in any of my undertakings. These handsome promises were likewise confirmed by the tom-tom beaters. The doctor and the collector, both of whom spoke English fluently, interpreted the Singhalese speeches, while their fellow-townsmen listened with eager attention, and curiously inspected the new arrival and his luggage.

This ceremonious reception was all the more amusing from the fact that the dress of the distinguished reception committee was a comical mixture of the fashions of Europe and Ceylon. The upper half of the person was clad according to the latest approved mode of the former country, and the lower half in strict accordance with the prevailing Singhalese styles. Beginning with the head, our eyes are delighted by a "chimney-pot" hat of irreproachable style —of all head-gear, without a doubt, the most hideous, as well as the most unpractical, but the Singhalese chief, whose observant eye has noticed that his European brother on all occasions of ceremony considers a head-covering of this sort an indispensable emblem of his high position as gentleman, would think it an unpardonable breach of etiquette were he to appear even in the hottest weather without the imposing "chimney-pot" when ceremony demanded it. His good-natured bronze face, which the narrow-brimmed hat scarcely shades, is framed by a heavy black beard that is cut away from the chin; below it protrude the points of a voluminous collar, around which is elaborately knotted a gorgeous silk kerchief. Nor is the black "dress-coat," with its concomitant white waistcoat, missing; the latter is profusely ornamented with brilliant stones and gold embroidery. Instead of the customary trousers, however, the dusky official wears the national covering for the lower extremities, a red comboy—a wide apron that reminds one of the red petticoats worn by the German peasant-girls. His dainty little feet are either entirely bare, or protected merely by sandals.

After the friendly reception, which certainly promised favorably for my stay in Belligam, my new protector led the way through the gate into the pretty rest-house garden, which is enclosed by a white wall. The first sight of my new abiding-place surpassed my expectations. The rest-house is a handsome, one-storied stone structure, with the usual wide portico, white columns, and projecting red tile roof. The broad green lawn stretching along the east front of the house is ornamented by a superb teak tree whose columnar trunk rises to a height of eighty or ninety feet. Leguminous climbers are twined about it and hang in graceful festoons from the lofty branches. On the south side of the lawn a couple of cows are peacefully grazing in the shade of the most magnificent bread-fruit trees, whose gnarled trunks and far-spreading branches call to mind the finest oaks of our northern climate; but the large, deeply-lobed, dark green and glossy leaves, as well as the huge, light green fruit, give them a far more imposing appearance.

Between the umbrageous crowns of these artocarpus giants is seen a smiling view of the sunny, almost circular harbor of Belligam, on which, at the moment, are numerous vessels in full sail returning from a fishing expedition. The rocky promontory opposite (to the south) is partly covered with jungle and partly with cocoa-groves; the huts of the fishing village of Mirissa dot its gleaming sands. In the harbor, scarcely two minutes distant from the rest-house, lies a charming rock islet, *Gan-Duva,* entirely covered with elegant cocoa-palms.

Continuing our voyage of discovery around the rest-house, we enter the fruit garden, which is filled with laughing bananas and manihots, and which extends from the west side of the house to a steep hill. At the foot of the latter is an out-building which contains the kitchen, and several store-rooms which will be of great service for my collections. A dense thicket, populated by apes and parrots, crowns the summit of the hill, whose steep slopes are decked with luxuriant shrubbery and a carpet of blossoming creepers. Fascinated by the charming situation and idyllic surroundings of the rest-house, and eager to inspect its interior, I ascended the broad stone steps leading to the front entrance. Here I was met by another salutatory (half English, half Pali) from the steward of my new abode, the aged rest-house keeper. With arms crossed on his breast, his bronze frame bent almost double, the old fellow came toward me, and in the most submissive manner hoped I would be satisfied with the simple accommodations of the rest-house; whatever of rice and curry, of fruits and fishes the village could supply, that should be provided for my entertainment; nor should there be a lack of willing service. In short, I was to have everything that would make me comfortable while I remained in Belligam. All this,'and much more was handsomely promised by the old man in a well-constructed speech that was flavored with a number of philosophical phrases. As I looked into his broad, good-natured face, with its short, turned-up nose, small eyes, thick lips, and long, tangled, silvery beard, there suddenly occurred to me the familiar bust of Socrates which always recalled the head of a satyr. This resemblance, and my inability to remember the interminable Singhalese name of my host, caused me to straightway dub him Socrates. The rechristening was amply justified later, for the old man proved himself in various ways a worthy follower of his illustrious Greek prototype.

And now it seemed as if the familiar impressions of classic antiquity which greeted me on the very threshold of my idyllic abode were to continue to haunt me. When Socrates conducted me across the portico into the wide entrance hall, there, with arms uplifted, in an attitude of supplication, stood a lovely nude bronze figure that could be no other than the celebrated statue of the boy at prayer, the "*Adorante.*" What was my surprise, to see this exquisite bronze image suddenly quicken, drop its arms, kneel at my feet, lift its eyes beseechingly to my face, then bow its beautiful head in mute submission until the long black locks lay on the stone floor.

The boy—so Socrates informed me—who was a member of one of the lowest castes, the Rodiya, had lost his parents when a mere child, and had been befriended out of compassion by the rest-house keeper. He was intended for my personal service, and would have nothing to do but wait exclusively on me; he was a good-natured lad, and would be sure to perform his duties faithfully. In answer to my request for the name of my page, Socrates informed me that it was, "Gamameda" (village-centre: *gama*, village; and *meda*, centre). Naturally Ganymede instantly substituted itself, for a nobler namesake of Jove's favorite than this lithe-limbed, symmetrical youth could not have been found. Besides, Gamameda soon developed a wonderful efficiency as cup-bearer. He would not allow any one but himself to open a cocoanut for me, or fetch me a glass of palm wine. I was therefore justified in changing his name, as well as that of his master. Among the many valued images that animate my recollections of this tropical paradise, Ganymede is one of the most highly prized. He not only performed his menial duties with extreme conscientiousness and attention, but he exhibited an attachment for my person and a readiness to serve me that was really touching. An unfortunate member of the Rodiya caste, the poor boy had from his infancy been subjected to the contempt of his fellows, and had been the object of constant unkindness and even cruelty; with the exception of old Socrates (who at times also treated him rather harshly), no one had taken kindly notice of him. Consequently my gentleness towards him from the very first moment was as novel to him as it was delightful. He was specially grateful for the following service: A few days before my arrival he had run a thorn deep into his foot; in drawing it out a fragment had broken off and remained in the wound. I removed it after considerable trouble, and treated the painful wound with carbolic acid so successfully that it healed in a short time. From that hour the grateful Ganymede followed me like my shadow, and sought to read my wishes in my eyes. Scarcely had I risen from my bed when he was beside me with a freshly-plucked cocoanut, from which he offered me a delicious morning drink. At table he never took his eyes from my face, and always anticipated my every wish. When at work, he would clean my anatomical instruments and the microscope lenses. But happy Ganymede, when we sallied out to the cocoa-groves, or the sea-shore, to sketch or collect, to hunt or fish. On such occasions, if I allowed him to carry the paint-box or photographic camera, to sling the gun or the botanical case over his shoulder, he would strut after me with a beaming face, and look proudly around at the wondering Singhalese, who saw in him only the despised Rodiya slave; to them such distinction was utterly incomprehensible. My interpreter, the grudging William, was especially aggrieved, and sought every opportunity to slander Ganymede, but soon found that I would not tolerate any injury to my favorite. Many of the handsomest and most valuable acquisitions in my collections I owe to the untiring zeal and skill of this despised Rodiya. With the keen eye, dextrous hand, and fleetness of motion common to the Singhalese children, he knew how to secure the soaring butterfly and the darting fish. When hunting in the forest, he would climb like a cat to tops of the tallest trees, or dart through the thickest jungle with a nimbleness that was truly marvellous.

Although the Rodiya caste to which Gamameda belongs, is of purely Ceylonese origin, it is regarded by the higher castes on the island (notwithstanding the fact that caste distinctions are not so rigid here as on the mainland) with as much abhorrence as the Pariahs in India. Its members perform only such labor as is considered degrading—to which, singularly enough, is reckoned the washing of clothes—and no Singhalese of higher caste will have any association whatever with a Rodiya.

As if kind mother nature wished to atone for the unjust treatment of her outcast children, she bestows on them not only the blessing of perfect contentment, but endows them with the graceful gift of beauty—a benefice that may be constantly admired, as the Rodiyas wear only the most necessary clothing.

The boys and young men, as well as the younger girls, are, on an average, more beautifully formed and of nobler feature than the rest of the Singhalese—circumstances which perhaps account for the envy and hatred of the higher castes.

As a general thing the stronger sex in Ceylon is also the handsomer, especially the youths, whose noble Aryan features are distinguished by a certain dreaminess of expression that is very attractive. Their delicate mouths are particularly beautiful, while their dark, soulful eyes are eloquent with promises their dull brains are unable to fulfil; added to these perfections is a perfectly oval face framed by luxuriant raven tresses. As neither boys nor girls wear clothes until their eighth or ninth year—or at most only a narrow cloth around the loins—they furnish the most suitable "life" for the Eden-like landscape; and the traveler frequently imagines he sees before him an animated Greek god. Ransonnet, on Plate IV., in his work on Ceylon, has a sketch of a fourteen-year-old Siniapu boy that illustrates the characteristics above mentioned. Ganymede is very like the sketch, only his features are even more delicate and girlish, and remind one of the lovely face of Mignon.

In old age the charm of this mild and attractive physiognomy is entirely lost—especially is this the case with the gentler sex—and a certain harsh expression or dulness takes its place. Frequently the bones of the face protrude, and give it anything but a pleasing appearance. A conspicuous illustration of this peculiar deformity was old Babua, the third personality presented to me in the rest-house of Belligam, in the character of its cook. The lean old fel ow with his shrivelled limbs bore no resemblance whatever to the rotund, corpulent personage who reigns in the kitchens of our imagination. He was more like the quadrumanous ancestors of man, and when the wide mouth in the skinny brown face was distended by a grinning smile the resemblance to an old ape became all the more striking. It was therefore a comical coincidence that *Babuin* should be the systematic name of a branch of the ape family (*Cynocephalus babuin*). Moreover, the old fellow, with his powerful under jaw, and low, receding forehead (perhaps from negro blood in his veins) was a very harmless and good-natured creature. His ambition was satisfied if he succeeded in discovering a new kind of curry as a concomitant to the dish of rice he daily set before me, and I praised the mess. I could have wished that he—as well as old Socrates—would have paid more attention to cleanliness in the primitive kitchen.

To the three permanent occupants of the rest-house was added a fourth ministering spirit in the person of William, my interpreter, whom I had brought with me from Galle. My English friends in the latter place had urged me to hire several servants: one to act as interpreter, one to assist me hunt, a valet, etc., etc.; but, having seen quite enough of the trouble and vexation a retinue of hirelings can create for their master, I did not take kindly to such a division of labor. I was very glad, therefore, to find that William could combine the functions of interpreter, huntsman, valet, and assistant in general. He had been a soldier, had served in the capacity of body-servant to an officer—and that he had done it well was conclusively proved by documentary evidence—was a tolerably skilful and willing fellow. Being a pure-blood Singhalese, however, he was endowed with the national aversion to work in general and manual toil in particular; he considered it mere prudence and wisdom to expend on every task he was called upon to perform as much time and as little energy as possible. All his interests and ambition—like most of the Singhalese youths—were centred in the artistic arrangement of his coiffure. To wash and comb, to dry and oil his long black hair, then to twist it into a perfectly regular coil, and fasten it with a large tortoise-shell comb at the back of his head, was for William a most important six-act drama, for the performance of which several hours every morning were required. To recover from the exhaustion to which these arduous exertions always reduced him, an additional hour or two was of course necessary. His duties as interpreter and valet were performed with scrupulous care; but he would indignantly refuse to degrade himself by labor which required a great amount of physical exertion: on such occasions he would assure me with extreme hauteur that he was no "cooly." His trifling domestic tasks were performed with tolerable neatness and dispatch, and he was always ready and willing to assist me with the microscope.

The fair and curious reader will doubtless inquire why I have not mentioned the feminine inhabitants of the Belligam rest-house. Unfortunately I am unable to say anything about them, for the simple reason that there were none there. Not only the cook, Babua, and the housekeeper, Socrates, and the maid, William, but the laundress that fetched my clothes every week, to beat them on the stones in the river, all were of the masculine gender, as are most of the servants in India. Nor was there much to be seen of the fairer sex in Weligama—but of this more hereafter.

XI.

A Zoological Laboratory in Ceylon.

My first task in Belligam was, with the assistance of the four ministering spirits, to establish myself as comfortably as possible in the rest-house, and to set up a zoological laboratory. The house contained three spacious apartments, of which the middle one—the dining-room—served as sitting-room for the casual guests (especially for the government officials who might happen to patronize the house); a large dining-table, two benches, and several chairs completed the furnishing. The large rooms adjoining the dining-saloon on either side were guest-chambers with huge Indian bedsteads, in which the restless dreamer might on his own axis comfortably describe a complete circle without touching the edges with his toes. The voluminous mosquito nets stretched over them doubtless once rendered excellent service, but at present only the evidences of past utility remained. I found the mattresses also in a condition that rendered it advisable for me to adopt the native fashion of sleeping on palm mats. In addition to the giant bedsteads in the guest-chambers, there was a small table with the necessary toilet appliances, and a couple of chairs. The long windows in the white walls were, as everywhere in the tropics, without glass, but could be closed by the green wooden jalousies. The floor was laid with flagstones. I selected the lighter chamber facing the south, from which, through the door opening on a veranda, there was a lovely view of the harbor. I would have preferred to use this room solely as a work room and zoological laboratory, and the one facing north as a sitting and bedroom; but one of them had to be reserved for travelers. The primitive simplicity of the rest-house furnishing compelled me to provide some additional and absolutely necessary household articles, without which it would have been impossible for me to accomplish my work.

First of all I required large tables and benches, as well as cupboards and chests of drawers. To procure these was by no means an easy task, and although my new friends assisted me to the best of their ability, my laboratory, when at last ready for occupation, lacked many things. The first chief had supplied me with boards which, when laid on my empty boxes, served as shelves for bottles and jars. The second chief gave me two old tables. The tax-gatherer (who, by the way, was a very polite and accomplished person) loaned me a pair of small cupboards, in which I could lock my valuable instruments, chemicals and poisons. The schoolmaster furnished a set of small book-shelves, and in this manner the laboratory was made tolerably practicable for my purpose by the worthy Belligamians, who desired nothing in payment for the small favors but the privilege of satisfying their curiosity. This, however, soon assumed such enormous proportions that it became extremely annoying and robbed me of much valuable time.

Aside from these most necessary household articles (which are considered superfluous luxuries by most of the Singhalese), I could procure little or nothing that would be of use to me in Belligam; I was therefore heartily glad that I had brought from Europe all the requirements for my domestic economy, as well as for my zoological investigations. True, there was in the village a so-called carpenter, also a species of locksmith whose services I might frequently have required. But the primitive character of their tools sufficiently proved the quality of workmanship I might expect from them.

It soon became evident that I would have to do everything for myself, for every time I called one of these Singhalese artisans to my aid I was obliged to remodel his work from the very beginning. As for letting them attempt to repair any of my instruments—and unfortunately they frequently needed it—it was entirely out of the question.

However, in spite of all hindrances I succeeded in a few

days in transforming the roomy guest-chamber into a fairly comfortable laboratory adequate to the requirements of our modern marine zoology. Microscopes and anatomical instruments were adjusted; a dozen large and several hundred small vials and jars were methodically arranged in rows on the shelves; the alcohol was decanted and the taste disguised with oil of turpentine, to preserve it from the bibulous inclinations of my servants. One of the two cupboards contained the domestic apothecary shop, as well as some fire-arms, ammunition, and the "magician's kitchen," which comprised the different micro-chemicals, photographic appliances, poisons for preparing and preserving animals, etc. In the other cupboard were stored books, papers, drawing materials, oil and water colors, and a number of valuable and fragile instruments. The legs of these two cupboards, as well as those of the tables, stood in earthen vessels, which were filled with water to protect them from the incursions of destructive ants and termites. Nets and fishing appliances occupied one corner of the room; guns and botanical cases another; in the third stood the soldering apparatus and tin boxes; while the fourth corner was entirely taken up by the huge bedstead which, during the day, served as a work table.

Along the walls were ranged the empty chests for the collections, as well as the tin boxes which contained my wearing apparel. Above them nails were driven into the wall on which to hang the barometer, thermometer, scales, and a number of articles of daily use. Thus, in a few days the rest-house of Belligam was made to look like the marine laboratory I had established for a six months' sojourn in Messina twenty-two years ago, and like the one on the Canary Island of Lanzarote fifteen years ago—with this difference: My zoological and artistic outfits this time were more complete and varied, while, on the other hand, the comforts of my domestic economy were much simpler and of a more primitive character. However, I was consoled for the lack of many conveniences, by the fact that I was only six degrees distant from the equator, and that no one in Ceylon had ever before enjoyed the use of so fine a laboratory for marine zoology—a thought that made me all the more eager to begin work.

The difficulties which attend labor of this sort in the

tropics, especially the subtle investigation of the structure and development of the lower marine fauna, are recognized and deplored by all the naturalists that have undertaken such tasks in the last decades. Consequently, I was prepared to meet with hindrances, but soon found that they were infinitely greater and of a more varied character than I had imagined. Not only the excessively hot and moist climate with all its destructive influences, but existence in an uncultured village, among a half-civilized people, as well as a lack of many accustomed conveniences of civilization, offer a thousand obstructions to the investigation and collecting of natural curiosities.

I often thought regretfully of the many advantages and conveniences which I had enjoyed while engaged in zoological studies on the Mediterranean shore, and which would be so sorely missed here.

One of the greatest difficulties was to find a serviceable boat, as well as skilled fishermen to man it. The peculiar canoes which attracted my notice when I arrived at Colombo, and which have already been described, are the only kind in use along the Ceylon coast, except, of course, in the harbors of the larger cities. These canoes, which are from twenty to twenty-five feet long, are so narrow that a grown person sitting in them cannot place his feet side by side. Consequently you are wedged as it were into these boats, which are aptly described as "leg-pinchers" by my friend Professor H. Vogel of Berlin, who has had occasion to use them. Another fault with these canoes is the characteristic outrigger which, while it lends security to the craft and prevents it from upsetting, also prevents it from turning quickly, and compels you to keep one side of the canoe always towards the shore, or the object you wish to approach. There is no rudder, and the propelling power is an oar which is used by the oarsman sitting in the end of the canoe, first on one side then on the other. The smaller canoes are manned by two, and the larger ones by four or six natives. In addition to the oar there is a low mast, to which is attached a large four-cornered sail. The latter renders excellent service in a fair wind, when the light canoe, whose narrow beam offers little resistance to the waves. glides like an arrow across the water. I have frequently traveled ten or twelve miles in an hour in one of these outrigger canoes—as rapidly as in a swift steam ship. Should the wind blow too vigorously, so that the boat careens too much to one side, the nimble boatmen clamber with ape-like dexterity along the slender outriggers, and squat on the balance-log to give it additional weight.

To dispose of a chest containing large glass jars, and the different instruments required to secure pelagic marine animals—especially *medusæ*—in such a craft was, of course, impossible. I was therefore obliged to construct a sort of platform on the canoe, on which I might sit comfortably or move freely about. On either end of the platform were the chests, containing bottles and jars of all sizes, securely fastened with coir ropes. Ropes of the same material are used to lash together the different parts of the canoe; indeed, the natives in building their boats use neither iron nor nails—only wood and cocoa fibre.

In effecting these improvements in my canoe, as well as in hiring and instructing the native boatmen, I was greatly assisted by the second head man of Belligam, the Arachy, *Abayawira*, to whom I am further indebted for other valuable services.

The government agent of the South Province had told me about the Arachy's superior qualifications, and had specially recommended me to his favor. I found him an unusually intelligent and enterprising Singhalese of perhaps forty years, whose interests and information lifted him far above the majority of his countrymen. There was none of that stupid indifference which characterizes most of the Singhalese, about the Arachy. He was keenly interested in education, and sought by every means in his power to further its advantages among his people. He spoke English fairly well, and expressed himself with a clearness and intelligence that frequently astonished me. Indeed the Arachy was even a philosopher—of a higher grade than old Socrates at the rest-house—and I remember with great pleasure the many and frequently very complex arguments we used to have on widely different subjects. Free from the superstitions and dread of spectres common to his Buddhist countrymen, and with a ready glance for the wonders of nature and their explanation by natural causes, the Arachy had developed into an independent free-thinker, and was delighted when he found that I was able to solve many of the problems which had sorely puzzled him. I can see him now, the dignified, handsome, bronze-hued man, with his expressive and regular features! How his black eyes sparkled with intelligence when I elucidated some natural phenomenon, and how his soft persuasive tones would plead for further enlightenment on this or that problematical question! In him I found all the good and commendable qualities of the Singhalese character, the gentle manner and natural reserve, developed in their most attractive form; and when I people the verdant paradise of my recollections with the slender forms of its native inhabitants, the Arachy and Ganymede ever appear side by side as ideal types of that enchanted realm. The Arachy's nephew, a well-informed young man of seventeen years or more, a student in the Colombo normal school, who was spending his vacation at Belligam, was also a very useful and agreeable companion. Assisted by him and the Arachy I was able to secure four of the best and most skilful fishermen in Belligam. I paid them five rupees for every expedition, and when they were required to dive to the coral banks, or when we were out on the water over half a day, I always added a couple of rupees to the sum agreed upon. At first I experienced considerable trouble with my uninitiated assistants, and when I dragged the fine-meshed pelagic net along the surface of the water, or showed them the tiny medusæ and polyps, the siphonophora and ctenophora, to secure which was evidently my main object, their looks plainly indicated that they thought me a lunatic. However, they gradually, and with commendable patience and indulgence, learned what it was I wanted, and then became quite as eager to enrich my collection with rare and beautiful specimens as I was myself. Two of the men were especially useful in diving to the coral banks; to their perseverance and ingenuity I am indebted for many of the lovely corals and curious animals native to the submarine gardens which I brought with me from Belligam.

But a more formidable obstruction to my pelagic fishing than the canoe and its crew, was presented by the tropical climate—that relentless and invincible enemy of the naturalist, who frustrates so many of his designs and baffles so many of his undertakings. This I was destined to experience the very first time I fished for marine treasures in the bay at Belligam. Detained by the numerous arrangements I was obliged to make for the expedition, I was not ready to depart for the fishing ground until nine o'clock. By that time the merciless tropical sun burned in the deep blue cloudless heavens with a radiance that transformed the perfectly smooth surface of the water into a gleaming mirror. The glare was intolerable to the eyes, and I was compelled to put on blue goggles if I wanted to keep them open. Hoping to find the temperature several degrees lower on the water I ordered my men to row quickly out; but the intense heat seemed rather to increase than diminish, while the dazzling mirror, unstirred by a breath of air, seemed a vast expanse of molten lead. Bathed in perspiration I fished for perhaps an hour when I became perfectly exhausted. My strength deserted me, there was a humming in my ears, while the increasing pressure on my temples made me apprehensive of sunstroke. As my clothes were already wringing wet with perspiration, I decided to try a remedy that had given me instant relief on similar occasions. I dashed a couple of pailfuls of sea water over my head, and covered it with a wet towel, on which I fastened my wide-brimmed sola hat. The result of this treatment was satisfactory, and I afterwards had recourse to it whenever the oppressive heat caused a return of the stupefying headache. With the water and the atmosphere both at a temperature of 22–26° R. such a drenching of the head with vaporable water is very beneficial. Even the wearing of wet clothes for several hours, which in our cool climate would give one a serious cold, is here as pleasant as it is harmless.

The first expedition on the Bay of Belligam convinced me that it abounded in pelagic animals of widely dissimilar classes. The jars into which the swimming inhabitants of the surface water were emptied from the gauze net were quite full after a few hours' fishing. Among thousands of infinitesimal crabs and *salpæ* floated delicate medusæ and siphonophora; multitudes of snail and mussel larvæ glided, by means of their dainty streamers, among fluttering sea-butterflies and Pteropoda; while hundreds of coral and crustacean larvæ were falling prey to rapacious arrow-worms. (*Sagitta*). The majority of these organisms are colorless and of the crystalline transparency of the sea-water in which they struggle desperately for existence. (According to Darwin's theory of selection, the transparent condition of these pelagic "glass-animals" is the result of this struggle for existence.)

Although some of the species found here were new to me, I was familiar with most of the genera, for the prolific Mediterranean—especially the famous Strait of Messina—furnishes just such pelagic curiosities when the conditions are favorable for surface-water fishing. Still, among the old acquaintances I met with in the Bay of Belligam, I noticed a number of new and attractive forms that provoked immediate microscopic observation. Consequently I ordered my men to row quickly back to the shore, and while we were scudding through the water I devoted myself to an examination my newly-acquired treasures. To my great disappointment I found at least half of the delicate captives dead and dying; some were overtaken by death in half an hour, others in less than fifteen minutes after they were taken from the bay. Their crystal bodies speedily clouded, and formed a white powdery mass on the bottom of the jars, and before we reached the shore I could detect the peculiar odor which proceeds from gelatinous bodies in a state of decomposition. In the Mediterranean, under similar circumstances, death is not followed by decomposition until after a period of five to ten hours; here, with a higher temperature by several degrees it took place in half an hour's time. Alarmed by this discovery I hastened our return to the land which we reached shortly before twelve o'clock. Here another difficulty presented itself: notwithstanding the midday sun's fierce heat, almost the entire population of Belligam was assembled on the strand to learn the result of my extraordinary method of fishing. Each one of the dusky throng wanted to see what I had caught, and wanted to know what I was going to do with it—or, rather, in what shape I was going to devour it; for, that sea-creatures were captured for any other purpose than a dietary one of course never entered their heads. Consequently the amazement of the inquisitive natives, among whom I made my way with great difficulty, was by no means small when they beheld merely the white sediment on the bottom of the large glass jars, and the few tiny pelagic creatures that were still actively disporting themselves in their new quarters. Afterwards the Arachy informed me that his fellow citizens could not understand, or indeed believe, that I was engaged in merely scientific work; most of them detected behind all this mysterious business some sort of witchcraft, the preparing of magic potions, etc, while the realistic Belligamians believed I was trying to invent a new curry. The still more enlightened were confident that I was simply a European lunatic.

Thus a valuable quarter of an hour was lost before I could force my way through the curious skeptics to the rest-house, and—as was my wont—to sort and distribute the thousand dainty creatures in glass vessels of fresh water.

By this time at least nine tenths of my treasures were dead, and among them the new ones whose forms had particularly interested me. The remaining tenth were already so exhausted that death seemed imminent at any moment, and in a few hours my jars were in fact nothing but huge receptacles for pelagic corpses! The following days I sought by every means to counteract the fatal influence of the tropical sun, but was only partially successful. It was simply impossible to maintain the necessary low temperature of the water. I was convinced that the first and most important requirements for the successful observation of marine fauna in so hot a country as Ceylon would be cool rooms and refrigerating water vessels. As large quantities of ice, which was formerly imported from North America, are now manufactured in Colombo by an artificial process at much less expense, it would not be a very difficult matter to arrange cool apartments, and refrigerated aquaria. But a considerable sum of money would be necessary for such a project, and that is not at my disposal. A second important requirement for successful zoological study in these refrigerated work-rooms would be glass windows—conveniences which are almost entirely unknown in Ceylon.

In the rest-house at Belligam, as well as in all the dwellings on the island, their place is supplied by wooden shutters or jalousies, at the top of which, as well as along the edges of the ceiling, and above the doors, are wide spaces to admit the air. For the purpose of ventilation these openings are of course very practical and comfortable, but for the naturalist, who is obliged to use a microscope, they

are as objectionable as detrimental. All sorts of winged
and creeping insects have free ingress; the most troublesome are the swarms of flies, gnats, ants, and termites.
Then the draught wafts your papers about, covers the instruments with dust, and frequently a more vigorous breeze dis-
places everything in the room. No less detrimental are the
jalousies themselves to a good light which is one of the
most important requisites for microscopic examinations—
especially when it is necessary to increase the magnifying
power. Very often the condition of the sun and wind
made it impossible for me to find a suitable corner for my
work-table—either in the darkened room, or on the all-too-
breezy veranda, whose wide, projecting roof was also a decidedly objectionable feature.

To these and various other local obstructions to zoological study, may be added the annoyances arising from the
curiosity of my neighbors. Never having seen any of the
wonderful instruments I had brought to their village, the
worthy Belligamians naturally wanted to know all about
them, what they were intended for, and how I used them.
In short, everything I did was for them a continual source
of amusement. Like all semi-civilized peoples, the Singhalese are in many respects mere children. Beneficent nature has made the conditions of their paradisal island so
favorable that the struggle for existence on it is comparatively easy, while actual toil is almost unknown. Innocent
games and chatter form their principal amusements, consequently every new object becomes a source of interest. The
too-frequent visits of my inquisitive neighbors at last became
such an intolerable nuisance that I was obliged to speak of
it to some of the more important personages in the village.
Steps were at once taken to remedy the evil; the masses
were excluded from the rest-house, but the visits of the important personages before mentioned became all the more
frequent and of longer duration. The "doctor" was especially interested in my microscope; the "tax-gatherer"
took a wonderful fancy to my paint-box; the "magistrate"
professed great admiration for the anatomical instruments
(as implements of torture, perhaps!); the "schoolmaster"
liked to examine my books, and so on. Everything I
owned was felt, tested, and examined a thousand times, and
quite as many nonsensical questions asked about each arti-

cle. Seeing how intensely curious my constantly increasing collections made the worthy Belligamians, I undertook to satisfy what I believed to be an earnest desire for information. At stated hours on certain days I delivered a series of formal lectures with copious illustrations—an expedient which had been employed with flattering success while fishing on the Mediterranean—but my native audiences would not believe half I told them, nor would they try to understand what I took great pains to explain. I soon became convinced that the childish inquisitiveness of the Singhalese had not yet developed into a true desire for knowledge, and that the causative coherence of phenomena had very little attraction for these innocent children!

It would weary the reader were I to enumerate allt he hindrances that opposed my zoological labors in the primitive laboratory at Belligam. Without the aid of a competent European assistant, I was obliged to depend entirely on my own exertions, and much valuable time was lost in the performance of extra work, which would not have been the case had I been engaged in a similar task on the European coast. Besides, the time I had to spend in Ceylon was entirely too short for the accomplishment of what I had originally intended: a series of coherent investigations of the history of evolution. Consequently, what I had at first deplored—that the number of new and peculiar sea animals in the Bay of Belligam was not nearly so large as I had expected—proved in the end a real consolation. The extensive marine investigations of the last twenty years (especially those conducted by the *Challenger* expedition) conclusively demonstrate, that the diversity of form among the inhabitants of the different oceans is nothing like so great as the difference between the inhabitants of the different continents. Of this fact my own investigations at Belligam were only additional proof. Of course I found a large number of new, and some very interesting animal forms—chiefly among the lower divisions of marine fauna—radiolarians, infusoria, sponges, corals, medusæ, and siphonophora—but they only furnished further evidence that the fauna of the surface-water of the Indian Ocean, as well as that along its shores, was closely allied to the better-known sea-animal world of the tropical Pacific Ocean; for instance, Philippine and Fiji Islands.

Other portions of the Indian coast may be richer in manifold and peculiar sea-animal forms than Ceylon, but the enormous quantity of rain which daily descends upon it would seem to me an extremely unfavorable circumstance. While the flora of the island owes its wanton exuberance to these deluging rains, they offer various obstructions to the development and prosperity of the fauna. The large masses of red earth which are daily carried into the ocean by the numerous streams, sully the purity of the water and diminish its saltness, thus destroying the pure, transparent quality of the sea water, which is one of the first conditions essential to the life of many marine, and particularly pelagic animals.

If in spite of all hindrances I amassed a considerable zoological collection in Belligam, and brought back to Jena far more material for study than I can hope to master in the remaining years of my life, then I owe the greater part of it to the indefatigable zeal of my faithful Ganymede, whose highest ambition was to enrich my collection with land and sea-creatures of all sorts. Through his influence a number of boys were engaged to collect for me, and the curiosity-trade with these little fellows soon assumed a very pleasant as well as profitable character. At stated periods a whole army of nude graceful lads would wait on me at the rest-house. One dusky little god would bring a pair of exquisitely-tinted fishes, another a curious sea-star or sea-urchin, a third would offer a huge black scorpion or milleped, a fourth would display a pair of gorgeous butterflies or beetles, and so on. The entertaining scenes always recalled similar ones I had enjoyed on the Mediterranean shore, especially at Naples and Messina. But how different the behavior of the little traders here and there! The Italian boys extolled their wares in loud, noisy tones, and with native eloquence frequently delivered long and flowery speeches eulogistic of their perfections. They asked ten times as much as the articles were worth, and were never satisfied even when I paid the exorbitant prices they demanded. On the other hand, the little Singhalese would shyly and respectfully lay their wares before me, and wait in silence to hear what I would offer for them. As a general thing they would be satisfied with a trifling coin, but they would be particularly delighted when I gave them any of the articles

I had brought with me from Europe for bartering purposes.

Unfortunately, I had neither time nor the appliances necessary to preserve all the interesting natural curiosities I collected in this manner. Here again the tropical climate and destructive insects presented insuperable difficulties—especially when I attempted to dry anything. To thoroughly dry organic substances in such a humid atmosphere is one of the most difficult problems, for even the very air is filled with moisture, and a specimen that is already dry will mould and slowly decompose. It is absolutely impossible to sufficiently dry many objects. Although I hung the skins of the birds and mammals I had shot and taken so much trouble to prepare in the sun for weeks, every night would thoroughly drench them with moisture.

More hostile still to the drying of natural curiosities than the humid atmosphere, are the legions of destructive insects. No place, no object, is safe from these pests. Even were there no chinks everywhere in the walls through which all sorts of creeping and flying beasties, as well as the humid air, have free ingress, it would still be impossible to protect one's self from their attacks. Nothing can withstand the assault of their powerful jaws; they will force an entrance through anything—the walls, the roof, and the stone floor, which they skilfully undermine. Frequently on rising in the morning one is astonished to find conical heaps of earth which have been flung up between the flagstones during the night by the industrious termite, or ant sappers and miners. I was convinced of the energy and dispatch with which these minute enemies accomplish their work before the end of my first month in Belligam. I had accumulated in these four weeks a handsome collection of dried butterflies and beetles, skins of birds and mammals, curious fruits and specimens of woods, ferns, and other interesting plants, and locked them—securely, as I imagined—in a small side-room of the rest-house. Almost every day I visited my treasures, to see whether the enemy had made any inroads upon them, and took good care always to destroy the advance-guard of the termite and ant armies I might find reconnoitring on my territory. By generous applications of camphor, naphtha, and carbolic acid I imagined I had sufficiently protected my treasures to leave them for a few days, as an excursion to a distant point, and some urgent work would require my attention for that length of time. How startled was I when at the end of the third day I entered my well-protected museum, and found most of my treasures transformed into heaps of dust and mould! A dozen regiments of large red ants had forced an entrance through the roof, several divisions of small black ants had entered through the walls, while a legion of termites had come up through the floor, and made a combined assault that resulted most disastrously for my collection!

From that moment I gave up collecting dried curiosities, and turned my attention to preserving in alcohol or Wickersheim fluid. The latter, which has been extolled beyond its actual merits, proved utterly useless. Even with alcohol I experienced considerable difficulty, for the supply I had brought from Europe was soon exhausted, and the domestic arrack (which is prepared by the natives) is of very inferior quality. The better alcohol obtainable in the larger cities is so very expensive—on account of the high tax on spirits—that I used it only in small quantities. Besides, much of my pleasure in these alcohol collections was spoiled by the disagreeable task of soldering the tin cases. Although the art is very simple—in theory—its practice is attended by considerable difficulty, especially in so primitive a village as Belligam. With the temperature at 22° or 24° R. it was actual torture to bend one's perspiring face over a red-hot stick of solder. I shudder when I think of the disagreeable labor which often tempted me to anathematize the whole collection! Of course these dearly-bought treasures are all the more valuable to me now. The thirty chests of natural curiosities accumulated in Belligam, and the twenty boxes full collected in Galle, amply reward me for all the tribulations I was obliged to endure.

XII.

Six Weeks among the Singhalese.

DAILY life in the rest-house of Belligam, after I had surmounted various obstacles, became very pleasant and satisfactory, and was attended by fewer objectionable features than I had at first apprehended. My four ministering spirits performed their tasks with tolerable diligence, and when anything was lacking my faithful Ganymede was always ready to supply the want. Fully awake to the prescribed limits of my time in Belligam and the many sacrifices I had made to this Indian journey, I would say to myself every morning when I awoke, "This day is worth at least five pounds sterling, and I must accomplish enough work to equal that sum in value." Accordingly I made it a rule not to lose a single hour, and especially to forego the pleasure of the customary siesta during the hot hours of noon; they would be my most fruitful working time, for I might be certain that no one would disturb me.

As Belligam is not quite six degrees from the equator, and even on the shortest day of the year there is scarcely an hour's difference between day and night, I might count on twelve working hours. Accordingly I arose regularly every morning before the sun, and had enjoyed my first refreshing bath when *Helios* made his appearance above the palm-groves on Cape Mirissa, directly opposite the rest-house. Then I would go out on the veranda, from whence I usually observed the sudden awakening of the young day, and find Ganymede awaiting me with a fresh cocoanut full of cool milk. In the mean time William would shake the millepeds, scorpions, and other unwelcome intruders from my clothes. Then Socrates would appear and humbly serve my tea, with the usual accompaniments of bananas and corn bread. I was obliged to forego the luxury of coffee, my favorite drink, for in Ceylon, whose coffee districts are its chief source of wealth, the noble beverage is usually so inferior that tea, which is much better, is generally preferred. The reason for this is said to be that the coffee bean cannot be properly dried on the island.

Usually at seven o'clock my boatman would fetch the nets and glass vessels for our daily expedition on the bay. On my return, after two or three hours, I would at once distribute the treasures I had secured in the different vessels prepared for their reception, and proceed to examine and preserve those animals which were still alive. The more important would be subjected to close microscopic scrutiny, and perhaps have their portraits sketched. Then

I would take my second bath, and after it, at eleven o'clock, a second meal, the so-called "breakfast," which consisted chiefly of the national "curry and rice." The rice itself was always simply boiled, but all the ingenuity stepmother nature had crammed into Babua's diminutive skull was daily exercised to surprise me with a new sort of curry. This most important ragoût-like mess, which always accompanied a dish of rice, would sometimes be "sweet" (that is, with very little spice), sometimes "hot" (sharp with cayenne pepper and the like pungent seasoning); again the indefinable "*mixtum compositum*," would be chiefly vegetable (cocoanut, and various other fruits and vegetables); then again it would be animal, with meats of different sorts. The latter always excited my liveliest wonder, for Babua seemed to think that because I was a zoologist I would of course be interested in all the different animal orders, and that their adaptability to a curry would form an important zoological problem which it would give me pleasure to solve. If on Monday the vertebrates would be represented in the curry by a delicate fish, on Tuesday the finer prawns and crabs would appear as types of the articulates. If on Wednesday cuttle-fish or calamary (*Sepia* and *Loligo*) would appear as the highly-organized representatives of the mollusks, they would be surpassed on Thursday by boiled snails, and occasionally baked oysters. On Friday would follow the remarkable tribe of echinoderms, represented by the egg-like sea-urchins, or the tough, leathery holothures (trepang). Saturdays I naturally expected to be regaled with plant-animals, and would look for corals, medusæ, or sponges, but my cook evidently held to the old-time theory which classes these zoophytes with plants, and substituted in their stead some sort of flying animal. Now it would be a bat or a bird, a corpulent rhinoceros-beetle, or a night-flying moth. Sundays a special feast would surprise me: the curry would contain an Indian fowl or else a plump lizard (iguana), occasionally also a snake that I at first took to be an eel. Babua was evidently sure of the near consanguinity of birds and reptiles, and thought it immaterial whether he prepared the younger or older sauropsida-form for the table. Fortunately for my European prejudices, I was familiarized by degrees with the zoological variety of the rest-house curry—though usually not until after I had resignedly swallowed the mess. Besides there was such a conglomeration of spices, roots, leaves, and fruits mixed up in the thick sauce that only the most minute anatomical examination would have enlightened me as to the nature of its component parts—and that I took good care not to undertake.

The first week in Belligam I doubted very much whether I could stand a curry and rice diet for two months. But I was like Goethe with the muddy "Merseburger beer:" at first I could hardly make up my mind to taste the curry, and afterwards I could hardly do without it. The second week I concluded to make virtue a necessity, and determined to find curry palatable—or at least interesting; and before the end of the first month gastronomic adaptation had made so thorough an Indian of me that I was constantly longing for new curries. I even devoted the results of my hunting expeditions to their discovery, and surprised old Babua himself with my improved curry-forms of ape and flying fox. The delicious fruits which graced the table at every meal richly compensated for the curry torments I had to endure. First of all I must gratefully mention the bananas, the noblest of tropical gifts that richly deserve their name of "paradise figs" (*Musa sapientum*). If this incomparable fruit in all tropical regions belongs to the most grateful of culture-plants, and repays its possessor a thousandfold for the trifling care bestowed upon it, then is this particularly the case in Ceylon. For is not this the "paradise of the lemur"? The pair of comical semi-apes or lemurs (*Stenops gracilis*) I kept at the rest-house were not in the least doubt about it; they preferred their luscious paradise figs to all other diet. Numerous varieties of the banana are cultivated by the Singhalese. The finest are the small golden "Lady-fingers," which are really not much larger than the finger of a fine lady, and are distinguished by a peculiar sweetness. The huge water banana is the shape, size, and color of a large cucumber, and contains a refreshing, thirst-satisfying juice. The thick potato banana is valued for its farinaceous substance and nourishing qualities, three or four being sufficient to satisfy hunger. The anana banana is distinguished by a delicious fragrance; the cinnamon banana by its spicy taste, etc. Usually the banana is eaten raw, but it is very palatable when fried in lard or baked. No other fruit on earth is at the same time so delicious to the taste and nourishing, so wholesome and abundant. A single banana tree will produce a cluster of fruit that contains several hundred bananas, and this tree, with its magnificent crown of huge green plume-like leaves, is merely an annual. The picturesque beauty of the banana vies with its inestimable utility. It is the loveliest adornment of the native huts. If I might transplant to my garden in Europe but one tropical plant, the "*Musa sapientum*" would certainly have the preference over all others. This "Muse of the Sages" is in truth a vegetable "Philosopher's stone."

Next to the banana—of which I consumed several at every meal—the mango (*Mangifera indica*) formed one of the principal adornments of the rest-house table. It is a green, egg-shaped fruit, from three to six inches long, with a cream-like, golden pulp that has a faint but pronounced turpentine aroma. I found the fruit of the passion-flower (*Passiflora*) very agreeable, and very similar to our gooseberry. I was less pleased with the celebrated custard-apple, the scaly fruit of the *Annona squamosa*, and with the Indian almond, the hard nut of the *Terminalia catappa*. The quality of the apple and orange grown in Ceylon is very inferior; the latter, which will not ripen, is juiceless and stringy. The inferiority of these and some other fruits is doubtless due to the want of cultivation. The Singhalese are too indolent to trouble themselves with the cultivation of plants. After I had refreshed myself with a simple breakfast I would usually devote the hottest hours of the day, from twelve to four, to anatomical or microscopic work, to observations and sketching, as well as preserving and packing collected material. The following hours, from four to six, I would devote to excursions into the country around Belligam; now I would sketch in water colors, now perpetuate a beautiful view by the aid of my photographic camera. Sometimes I would go into the forest to shoot apes and birds, or collect snails and insects; and sometimes I would hunt for rare curiosities among the coral reefs along the shore. Usually about an hour before sundown I would return richly laden with spoil to the rest-house, when another hour would be spent in attending to the objects I had collected: skinning and preparing the animals I had shot, pressing plants, etc. Thus it would be eight o'clock before I was ready for dinner, the second meal of consequence. Here again the chief dish would be the inevitable "curry and rice." It was followed by fish or crabs, both of which I relished immensely. Then followed farinaceous dishes, after which delicious fruits concluded the meal. Belligam is of course well supplied with fish of all sorts. One of the finest is the Seir fish (*Cybium guttatum*), a large flat thorny finned fish belonging to the mackerel or *Scomberidæ* family. The *Cataphracti*, *Squamipennes*, and *Labroides* families also furnished savory representatives. Less deserving of praise were the curious ray-fish and sharks, of which huge examples were daily exposed for sale in the fish-market. In trying to render these "primary fishes"—the ancestors of the higher vertebrates (man included)—palatable by pungent pepper sauces, Babua evidently reckoned on the peculiar philo-genetic interest they might have for me.

From this *ménu* the indulgent reader may infer that I was in a fair way of becoming a vegetarian. True, Socrates on several occasions sought to delight me with what he considered extra dainties: beefsteak and mutton chops. But I forbear to mention my suspicions concerning the true nature of the animal to which I was indebted for these special delicacies.

The lack of European meat diet was occasionally supplied by the results of a successful hunting expedition. First among the relishes thus obtained was roast ape; this noble game is exceedingly palatable either roasted or stewed in vinegar. The flesh of the flying fox is not so appetizing; it has a peculiar musk-like odor. The flesh of the giant lizard (*Monitor dracæna*) can scarcely be distinguished from veal; while the snake soup is very like a soup made of eels. Among the various birds which were used as substitutes for domestic fowl were wild pigeons and ducks, crows and herons. If to these are added the different "*frutti di mare*"—the piquant fruits of the sea—mussels, snails, sea-urchins, holothures, etc., the bill of fare at Belligam may be said to offer a greater variety than one would at first suppose.

In addition to these native products Mr. Scott had

kindly furnished me with all sorts of European conserves, Scotch marmalade, Liebig's extracts, etc., as well as a generous supply of liquors. At first the important question of what to drink seemed a difficult one to answer. Although the highlands of Ceylon are abundantly supplied with pure spring water, the drinking water of the lowlands is bad and very unwholesome. The copious rains which deluge the island every day wash masses of earth and vegetable remains into the rivers, whose waters in many places communicate with stagnant lagoons. Consequently the water used for drinking purposes is always boiled, made into weak tea, or mixed with wine or whiskey. My friend Scott had sent me a generous quantity of the latter beverage, but I preferred cocoanut milk, which I found agreeable and refreshing as well as wholesome.

My frugal dinner happily over, I would ramble along the deserted seashore, or enjoy the illumination of the cocoa-grove by the myriads of glow-worms and fireflies. Then I would write a few lines in my note-book, or try to read by the dim light of my cocoa-oil lamp. Usually by nine o'clock extreme weariness would compel me to seek my couch—after the clothes-shaking process of the morning had been repeated. The large black scorpions (six inches long) are so numerous that I once collected a half dozen in an hour's time. Snakes also abound in great numbers. The pretty green whip-snakes hang everywhere from the branches of the trees, and huge rat-snakes (*Coryphodon blumenbachii*) at night chase the rats and mice over the roof. Although they are perfectly harmless it is by no means a pleasant sensation to have a snake five feet long suddenly drop through a hole in the roof, and occasionally on your bed. However my nights were rarely disturbed by the various beasties of Belligam, except occasionally by the howl of a jackal, the dismal cry of the devil-bird (an owl, *Syrnium indrani*), or some other night bird. The tinkling notes of the dainty little tree frog, whose habitat is in the cup of a large flower, was a soothing lullaby. More frequently the play of my own thoughts would drive slumber from my eyes. Recollections of past experiences and enjoyments and anticipations of those to come would crowd my brain. In long and brilliant succession the motley scenes of the past weeks would flit before me, and captivating plans for the morrow be devised. My attempts at photography and sketching in water colors, as well as my work in the zoological laboratory, gradually brought me into closer relations with the bronze-hued Belligamians, the majority of whom are pure Singhalese. The very first week of my sojourn in the village I was called upon to assist the "native doctor" perform several surgical operations, which were happily successful. My reputation as skilled surgeon soon assumed such exaggerated proportions that I would gladly have transferred the brilliant (if not profitable) practice to one of my worthy colleagues in Germany. I was even reputed to be a conjurer that could brew magic potions from certain plants and extract gold from different sea animals. The most astonishing demands were made on my black art. Old and young would follow me in crowds whenever I rambled through the village or its surroundings, and behold in everything I did some mysterious witchcraft.

As I mentioned before, the trade in natural curiosities became a very interesting and profitable feature of my residence in Belligam. Among the various articles of barter I had brought with me, the iron instruments, knives, scissors, tongs, hammers, etc., were especially coveted; also glass beads, colored stones, and similar articles of adornment. But the highest worth was given—and it speaks well for the artistic perceptions of the Singhalese—to the highly-colored illustrations, of which I had brought two or three hundred. These works of art, the familiar favorites of our children (the celebrated *Bilderbogen aus Neu-Ruppin, Schön zu haben, bei Gustav Kühn; Stück für Stück, fünf pfennig!*), met with an exceedingly favorable reception in Belligam, and I was only sorry that I had not laid in a larger supply. As gifts to the important personages they were also very acceptable, and I could offer nothing better in return for the heaps of cocoanuts, bananas, mangoes, and other luscious fruits which were daily sent to the resthouse. Soon all the more imposing huts in the village were decorated with one or more of these productions of German art. Indeed, several chiefs from neighboring villages brought me offerings of fruit and flowers in order to secure some of the coveted pictures. The subjects most approved by my dusky patrons were those appurtenant to the military: Prussian ulans, Austrian hussars, French artillery, English marines, etc. The second choice embodied theatrical scenes, such as Titania and Oberon, The White Lady, Somnambula, and Wagner's Nibelungen Ring. The third choice comprised domestic animals: horses, cows, sheep. The fourth and last was for *genre* pictures and landscapes, the more gorgeous the better.

This mutual present-giving soon established the friendliest relations between me and the inhabitants of Belligam; and when I walked or rode in my bullock cart through the village I was constantly bowing right and left in response to the respectful salutations of my dusky friends. In my walks through the Singhalese villages I was always struck by the absence of the fair sex; even among the children playing in the streets the boys formed by all odds the greater number. The girls are early accustomed to household work; they fade very young, are married at ten or twelve years of age, and become old women at twenty or thirty. Grandmothers of twenty-five and thirty are not infrequent. A further significant fact is the disproportion between the male and female births: ten boys on an average are born to eight or nine girls. Here the fairer sex is in the minority, and it is also the least attractive. The disproportion between the sexes is due, to some extent, to the remarkable institution of Polyandry. In spite of the efforts made by the English Government to suppress this custom it is still practised, and is probably increasing—particularly in the more remote parts of the island. It is not unusual to find two or three brothers with one wife in common, and there are ladies who rejoice in the possession of from eight to twelve husbands. These complicated family relations and their consequences form the theme of many extraordinary stories, but it is of course difficult to separate fact from fiction.

Old Socrates, with whom I once discussed the custom of Polyandry, astonished me by a novel theory of transmission that is sufficiently remarkable to be mentioned here. Although it is not to be found among the different laws of transmission, mentioned in the ninth chapter of my *Natural History of the Creation*, it is so original that the followers of Darwin cannot help but be interested in it. First, I must premise that Socrates was a son of the Kandyan highlands, and—according to his account—a worthy member of the highest caste. Consequently, he looked with supreme contempt on the inhabitants of Belligam, among whom he had lived for several years, and with whom he was plainly not on friendly terms. The very first day he warned me to beware of them, and enumerated a number of their most repulsive faults. "Of course," he added abruptly, shrugging his shoulders, "their baseness is not to be wondered at; for you must know, sir, that every one of these lowland people had several fathers, and as a number of evil qualities was inherited from every one of the sires, the deterioration of the race is quite natural!"

Such universal depravity of course made me doubtful as to the propriety of remaining in Belligam, but I was assured by the worthy steward of the rest-house that *he* was to be trusted, and that I might confidently depend on his being a perfectly upright and honest man. I was considerably surprised when, shortly afterwards, the first head man called on me, and in the strictest confidence repeated almost the same words. I was enlightened as to the real character of the Belligamians after I had heard the same story, with different variations, from the half dozen or more important personages whose visits followed that of their chief.

The shadow which these remarkable communications cast on the imaginary paradisal innocence of the untutored Singhalese, became all the more gloomy when the "judge" (or, as he preferred to be called, the "President of the Chamber of Justice,") informed me with a sigh that he had to work harder than any one in the village, and that his judicial labors occupied the entire day. Indeed, I found the hall of justice (an open shed like the schoolhouse) almost always filled with villagers intent upon securing their rights. It was rather comforting to hear that a majority of the cases were slander, cheating, and stealing—particularly the latter. An inherent partiality for what does not belong to him characterizes the Singhalese. He is also a liar of the highest degree, but no friend of violent deeds. Corporeal injuries and manslaughter are of infrequent occurrence. Murder is almost unknown. In fact the more active passions rarely appear; the Singhalese temperament is, on the whole, decidedly phlegmatic.

The Singhalese are extremely fond of music and dancing,

both of a kind that would be little to the European taste. The principal instruments are drums and tom-toms, vigorously beaten with wooden clubs, reed-pipes, and a primitive instrument with a single string (monochord). Evenings, when I heard the ear-splitting noise of these instruments, and would follow the sound, I would be sure to find before a fire, under a group of palms, a troop of a half dozen or more naked brown fellows who had fantastically painted themselves with white, yellow, and red stripes, jumping about and cutting the most extraordinary capers. Around them in a wide circle squatted the delighted audience, watching the grotesque performance with the greatest interest. About Christmas time (which is also the Buddhist New Year) these evening "devil-dances" are of more frequent occurrence, and are of peculiar religious signification. The principal performers then are fantastically decorated with colored feathers, wear horns and long tails, to the great delight of the village youth. Whole troops of these jumping and howling demons, accompanied by music, parade through the village all day long, while the nightly revels frequently develop into unseemly orgies.

A peculiar Buddhist feast had been prepared on the 19th of December by the chief of Dena-Pitya, a neighboring village. I was invited as a guest of honor, and was escorted to the festal scene by an imposing procession of Dena-Pityans. A dozen old, close-shaven Buddhist priests in yellow gowns received me under the branches of an immense sacred fig tree, and conducted me, amid the most extraordinary chanting, into the temple, which was tastefully decorated with wreaths and garlands. Here, the large image of Buddha, also profusely adorned with fragrant blossoms, was shown to me, and the signification of the paintings on the walls (scenes from the life of the god) amply expounded. Then I was conducted to a throne that had been prepared for me under a shady group of banana trees opposite the temple, and now the real performance began. A band of five tom-tom beaters and as many pipers began an uproar which was enough to move the rocks; at the same moment two dancers on stilts twelve feet long made their appearance and performed the most wonderful evolutions. At intervals the daughters of the chief, black-haired, voluptuous girls from twelve to twenty years old, carried around the refreshments: toddy or palm wine in cocoanut shells, sweetmeats and fruits. Unfortunately I could not understand a single word of the flowery oration delivered to me by the chief, but I guessed its purport to be the honor I had conferred on Dena-Pitya by my visit. The same was expressed in pantomime by a band of ten naked, gaudily-painted, and fantastically-adorned devil-dancers that capered madly around my throne. When at last towards sundown I took leave of my entertainers, and sought my bullock cart I found that it had been filled to overflowing by the hospitable Dena-Pityans with the most beautiful bananas and cocoanuts.

Scarcely was my rôle of honored guest at a genuine Buddhist feast concluded when the very next day I was called on to perform a similar part in the annual festivities of the Wesleyan Mission at Belligam. The following morning (Dec. 20th) the president of the mission at Point de Galle unexpectedly made his appearance at the rest-house, and informed me that a distribution of prizes among the scholars of the mission school at Belligam would take place that day, and that I could render no greater service to the good cause than by distributing the prizes among the children. In spite of all resistance I was at last obliged to yield. If I had rendered homage yesterday to immortal Buddha, to-day I must pay due respect to the excellent Mr. Wesley. Accordingly, in the afternoon I repaired to the public schoolhouse where perhaps one hundred and fifty children dressed in white were assembled; some were from Belligam, and some from the neighboring villages. The exercises began with a number of hymns—a performance that did not impress me very favorably with the musical abilities of the dusky schoolmaster. To me it seemed as if the one hundred and fifty children (about ninety boys and sixty girls) sang at least fifty different melodies, and atoned for the want of harmony by the strength of their voices. The examination in biblical history and English grammar which followed was very satisfactory, as were also the specimens of drawing and writing—especially when all the circumstances of this Ceylon paradise were considered. Then the Reverend Mr. N. delivered a formal lecture, at the conclusion of which he asked me to distribute the thirty prizes among the most diligent scholars. As I called the names from the list he gave me, the fortunate little Singhalese would come forward with beaming faces, and, bowing low before me, receive the reward for their industry, an English book or an illustrated primer. The ceremonies concluded with an entertainment of coffee and cakes. My friends in Galle and Colombo, whom the newspapers informed of my extraordinary performances, were greatly amused.

But the most remarkable celebration I attended while in Belligam was the burial of an aged Buddha priest on the 13th of January. While the common people here are simply buried (in the gardens behind their houses, or in the nearest cocoa-grove), the priests alone share the honor of being consumed by fire. The priest to be burned on this occasion was the oldest and most distinguished in the community; accordingly the funeral pyre of palm stems was erected near the principal temple. After the body, which rested on a flower-adorned bier, had been carried, amid solemn chanting, through the village, a band of young Buddha priests in yellow robes hoisted it to the top of the funeral pile which was about thirty feet high. The four corners of the pyre were supported by four cocoa-palms, between which was stretched canopy like a large white cloth. After the conclusion of various ceremonies, solemn dirges and prayer, the pile at five o'clock was lighted amidst the most deafening tom-tom uproar. A crowd of several thousand people watched the burning pile with expectant interest, and when the flames seized and devoured the muslin canopy a loud, jubilant cry went up from every throat—the soul of the burning priest had taken its flight to heaven. This was the signal for the inauguration of more cheerful ceremonies. Rice cakes and palm wine were distributed among the crowd, and a merry carousal followed that was kept up around the burning pyre the greater part of the night.

Aside from these celebrations and several excursions into the more distant parts of the country around Belligam, the pleasant routine of my retired life was seldom interrupted. Now and then an English Government official on a tour of inspection would spend a few hours, or the night at the rest-house. Less agreeable visitors were several Singhalese schoolmasters who had been attracted by the reputation of my laboratory. They came from a distant part of the province, introduced themselves as colleagues of mine, and wanted to know and see everything I could tell and show them. Of course I am only a schoolmaster myself, and cherish an unbounded reverence for my caste; but the peculiar species of the *Præceptor Singhalensis* with which I came in contact here was, I confess, very little to my taste. I was heartily glad when the importunate and conceited as well as ignorant fellows took their departure. Later I made the acquaintance of several more agreeable and better-informed examples of the same genera.

The most remarkable of all the numerous visits I received while in Belligam surprised me about Christmastime. I returned late one evening very tired from a distant excursion to Boralu, and was met at the gate in front of the rest-house by Socrates, who informed me in a mysterious whisper that four strange "ladies" were waiting to see me. Sure enough, in the dimly-lighted dining-room I found four representatives of the gentler sex, clad in European costume, but with execrable taste. I was considerably startled when the flickering lamp-light revealed four wrinkled old faces— each homelier than the other. Had there been but three I should have at once decided that my visitors were the three *Phorkyades* from the classic *Walpurgisnacht*, and— after the manner of Mephistopheles—would have made some flattering remarks. But this was spared me by the eldest of the four bronze graces (she was at least fifty!) rising and saying, in a polite, dignified manner and fairly good English, that she and her sisters were the knowledge-seeking daughters of a neighboring chief, and that their great-grandfather had been a Dutchman. They were greatly interested in science, and were anxious to inspect my collections, instruments, etc. I begged them to come again the following day, when I would gratify their thirst for information.

XIII.

Basamuna and Mirissa.

The immediate surroundings of Belligam, as well as the more distant hill country, abounds in enchanting pictures, and displays the idyllic and at the same time magnificent tropical character of South-west Ceylon in its greatest perfection. The numerous excursions I made in different directions, generally in company with Ganymede and William, are among my most agreeable recollections.

The lovely harbor of Belligam in situation, extent, and outline is almost exactly like that of Point de Galle; only the former is about one third the larger. Both harbors form a half-circle that opens towards the south, and is sheltered on either side by a rocky promontory. The radius of the half-circle at Belligam is perhaps something more than a nautical mile; at Galle it is a trifle less. The distance from promontory to promontory at the mouth of the Galle harbor is a mile and a half; at Belligam, only one mile. The westerly projection, which in Galle is occupied by the fort, in Belligam forms Basamuna Point—an exceedingly picturesque group of hills whose dark red cliffs are ornamented with clumps of the most remarkable pandanus trees. The eastern promontory, which in both places juts farther into the ocean and is the higher, in Galle contains the "watering-place," and in Belligam the charming groves of Mirissa.

The striking resemblance between these two bodies of water is increased by the similarity of their white sand beaches, both of which are shaded by magnificent cocoa-groves, and interspersed with red and brown rock masses. Here and there you catch a glimpse of the blue mountains in the distant highlands; among them the ever-conspicuous landmarks, the Haycock and Adam's Peak. Even in their wonderful coral formation are Galle and Belligam harbors alike.

As the largest and finest coral banks of Galle encircle the fort at the foot of the westerly promontory, so in Belligam they surround the craggy foot of Basamuna. The coral banks of Belligam are not so extensive as those of

Galle, but its harbor is much deeper and less obstructed by dangerous reefs. It is therefore difficult to understand why the splendid and commodious harbor of Belligam has not long ago become important for navigation, and why a proud and flourishing commercial city has not taken the place of the insignificant fishing village. Had I to establish a colony in India I would go nowhere else but to Belligemma!

Basamuna Point was my favorite promenade while I remained in Belligam. Afternoons, between four and five o'clock, after I had finished my zoological tasks, and carefully disposed of the marine treasures in alcohol which I had secured during the morning, I would hastily lock the microscope and anatomical instruments in their cupboard, and sling the cartridge box and botanical case around Ganymede's shoulders. William would carry the gun and butterfly nets, and I would take charge of the water-color utensils and sketch-book. The Basamuna cliffs are only half a mile distant from the rest-house, which, by the way, stands at the southern extremity of the village on the western side of the bay. The nearest way to the point is along the strand, past some isolated fishing huts, and then along the verge of the cocoa-forest. Here the incessant motion of the sea undermines the loamy shore, and every year causes the destruction of many noble cocoa-palms; their bleached corpses protrude from the water, and the brown root-tufts at the end of the stems, uplifted and washed clean by the waves, look like so many hairy heads. A multitude of crabs, common and hermit (*Ocypode* and *Pagurus*) animate the sands; here the latter do not bury their hinder parts in the deserted shell of the sea-snail, but prefer the more stately, red-lipped habitation of the large palm-snail (*Helix hæmastoma*). When the ebb tide is very low one may clamber around the foot of the steep cliffs at the point, over the exposed coral rocks, among which the receding waters have left a number of interesting sea animals: snails, mussels, sea-urchins, and stars. When the tide is in one must go through the palm-grove, in which are scattered native huts with their usual adornments of breadfruit and banana trees.

Emerging suddenly from the grove you are surprised by the utter solitude and wildness of the scene before you:

there are the dark red porphyry cliffs of Basamuna Point, savage crags, rent and cloven, at whose foot the raging surf flings its foamy spray high into the air. The crown of the rocky ridge is almost covered with screw-palms or pandanus shrubs, of such fantastic shapes and grotesque grouping that only the wildest fancies of a Gustave Doré could equal them. Like powerful serpents their stems curve and twist about each other, below resting on multitudes of long slender roots, above branched and forked like candelabra, their jagged arms uplifted towards heaven as if in imprecation, each arm terminating in a screw-shaped tuft of leaves. By the light of the full moon this ghost-like company with its long weird shadows is indeed a startling sight, and one can readily understand why the superstitious Singhalese cannot be persuaded to approach it. I must confess that even I—notwithstanding the assuring presence of a double-barrelled gun and a revolver—felt decidedly uncomfortable once between ten and eleven o'clock at night when I clambered around in this witch-like thicket, all the more so because Ganymede had piteously besought me not to venture near it. A brisk west wind flung the silvery foam of the surf with a noise like thunder high against the sombre cliffs, and chased a whole host of gloomy clouds across the sky. The fleeting shadows of these clouds and the magical light of the full moon, gave to the quivering foliage and tangled branches an effect than which it would be impossible to imagine one more uncanny.

After you have forced your way through the pandanus thicket, and walked out on the projecting cliffs at the point, you will see on your left the entrance to Belligam Bay, and far to the south the cocoa-palms of the distant Mirissa Point; on the right you will behold a graceful curve of shore fringed with palms, and beyond another rocky point which juts into the water to the north of this stretch of beach, a lovely island overgrown with shrubbery. Of the village from which we are separated by several wooded hills there is nothing to be seen, and no trace of human existence mars the impression of absolute seclusion and solitude that lingers about this enchanted ocean-lookout. Free and unhindered the glance from here flies across the immeasurable stretch of water, and meets with *terra firma* only after it has traveled thirty degrees towards the west, a land that in every particular is the antipode of our luxuriant surroundings—the arid, plantless coast of the Abyssinian Somali negroes. But our thoughts will fly still farther towards the north-west, for the radiant sun bends lower and lower towards the violet horizon, and the witching hour of eve draws near; "*die hehre Stunde, da mit stillem Sehnen der ferne Schiffer an die theure Heimath denkt.*" Homeward fly our thoughts to dear Thuringia, and to all the faithful hearts now gathered around the evening lamp or cheerful fire, and perhaps speaking of the wanderer in distant India, while deep snows cover the hills and valleys with a fleecy mantle. What a contrast to our surroundings! The glowing sun now sinks into the ocean and floods the red cliffs on which we stand with a veritable sea of flame. How delicate and airy are the rosy evening clouds, and how lovely the gilded strand with its fringe of stately palms! But we have scarcely time to follow the brilliant play of color, its rapid change of tints, when it has vanished, and the brief twilight follows so quickly in its wake that it is quite dark before we have carefully wended our way through the palm-grove back to the rest-house.

Similar and yet different from the attractions of Basamuna are those of the opposing point, charming Mirissa. To reach this point in a sail-boat requires, if the breeze is favorable, less than a quarter of an hour; but if you walk along the shore around the bay several hours are necessary, for you will have to cross the mouth of the Polwatta River, which flows into the bay at its north-east corner. It was a wonderfully bright morning (Jan. 6th), when I sailed across to Mirissa, supplied with provisions for the whole day, as I expected to make several excursions from that point. The little fishing village of Mirissa—the "mussel-village" which stretches along the foot of the promontory, takes its name from the multitudes of mussels and oysters which cover the rocks along the shore. A large shoal of fish (similar to the anchovy) engaged the attention of the inhabitants as we approached the village. All the available canoes were distributed among the shoal, and old and young were busy with small hand-nets securing as many fish as possible. We doubled the picturesque cape, against whose mighty cliffs the surf dashed furiously, sailed a mile or so farther along the shore, and landed in a sheltered little cove. Accompanied by Ganymede I climbed to the top of the promontory, and rambled through the beautiful grove, whose stately trees (chiefly cedars and terminalia) were festooned with exquisite climbing plants. Numerous apes and parrots enlivened the grove, but they were too shy for me to get a shot at them. When towards midday we returned to the shore, I noticed near the boat a group of natives; the stately chief at their head, a handsome man of perhaps forty years, with a gentle, prepossessing countenance, approached me, and in the most respectful manner presented me with a basket that was filled with mangoes, bananas, oranges, and other noble fruits from his garden, and wreathed with fragrant jasmine, plumiera, and oleander blossoms. With as much cordiality as modesty he begged me to eat my lunch in his hut instead of under the cocoa shade on the shore. After I had thanked him and accepted his hospitable offer he sent some of his people forward to prepare for me, while William and two of my boatmen followed with our provisions. I myself took a refreshing bath in the ocean.

In about an hour the chief returned accompanied by a number of the prettiest children, who were adorned with flowers, and led me along a winding path through the cocoagrove to a part of the village I had not noticed before. Through a neat garden whose path was strewn with flowers we reached the chief's rather imposing residence, built entirely of bamboo canes, and covered with palm leaves. The entrance was decorated in the manner so well understood by the Singhalese with ornaments of braided palm splints. Under the projecting roof, which formed a shady veranda in front of the hut, a large table had been improvised of palm stems and boards, and covered with fresh banana leaves. On it was tastefully arranged the luncheon we had brought from the rest-house, together with large dishes of rice and curry, fresh oysters, bananas, and cocoanuts— the gifts of our generous host. The splendid appetite with which I attacked these tempting viands (it had been sharpened by my long ramble and refreshing bath in the sea) was not in the least diminished by the fact that, during the entire meal, the chief's numerous family stood around the table and watched my every movement with intense interest, while the rest of the bronze-hued villagers looked on with equal interest from their more distant station in the garden.

At the conclusion of this original repast, which had been nectar and ambrosia to my keen appetite, my friendly host requested me to inscribe my name and that of my country on the palm leaf he had fastened above the doorway. Then he introduced his family—at least sixteen children, each one prettier and more attractive than the other. The older ones alone were partly clad, while the younger members of the family wore merely a piece of twine around the loins, on which, in front, hung a silver coin symbolical of clothing. Arms and legs were ornamented with silver bangles.

Here I beheld the most perfect types of the Singhalese form, and the sight was all the more interesting from the fact that the inhabitants of this part of the coast are famous for their pure, unmixed Singhalese blood. The elegant and voluptuous forms of the elder girls, whose feet and hands were conspicuously small, represented a large proportion of the thirty-two attributes which, according to the Singhalese poets, are necessary for perfect beauty—above all long, black, curly hair, almond-shaped eyes, swelling lips, bosom like young cocoanuts, etc. The complexion is cinnamon-brown in all its different shades; the younger children are the lighter. The fortunate mother of these sixteen handsome children (a stout smiling matron of perhaps forty) was highly gratified when William interpreted for her benefit the æsthetic admiration I expressed for her domestic felicity.

In the afternoon the chief and his elder sons conducted me to a small Buddha temple, some distance from the village, beside which stands a Bo-tree said to be very ancient. I found this specimen of the sacred fig a magnificent fellow indeed, beside whom all the rest of the trees in the grove were but mere saplings. His mighty trunk branches into two powerful arms, from whose shoulders depends a lovely green mantle of lianas. Other closely-interwoven climbers cover his trunk, beside which the diminutive temple looks like the habitation of a dwarf. The grounds around it are embellished with ornamental plants, among which the singular *Amorphophallus* is conspicuous by its crimson spadix and huge tuft of tattered foliage.

It was late in the afternoon before I returned to Mirissa, where I found another repast of bananas and cocoa milk awaiting me. The entire population escorted me to the shore, where I reluctantly bade adieu to my generous hosts, who, during our brief acquaintance, had exhibited all the most amiable qualities of the Singhalese character. I was very sorry I had not brought some picture books with which to emphasize my gratitude more substantially; in lieu of them I presented the chief with a pocket-knife and one of the large jars I had with me for the reception of captured sea animals. Shortly before sundown we again doubled Mirissa Point, and at the entrance to Belligam harbor were greeted by a sight I shall never forget. On the eastern shore of the harbor, above Mirissa Point, towers, bastion-like, a row of perpendicular cliffs, of shapely form, whose reddish tint, even in the customary light of day, vies with the intense hue of fresh-baked bricks. From them is derived the local name of the bay, the "Red Bay" of the ancient charts. Now, in the light of the setting sun, they glowed like coals of fire, while their shadows were the most brilliant cobalt blue. I understood why the Mirissa people spoke of them as the "red lamps," "*Ratu-Pana*". The eastern sky above these rocks of fire was a pale green, while the cloud masses heaped along the horizon were tinted with the most exquisite roseate hues. Add to these the warm brown of the cocoa and pandanus groves, the deepest, darkest green and violet of the shimmering water, and you have a color-concert of the highest class, such as I never saw before and never expect to see again. The hasty color-sketch I made of it while in the boat will serve merely to recall the magnificent spectacle, and yet what would the Berlin art-critics say to such a display of color?—those wise judges who condemn every picture that fails to conform in coloring and composition to the meagre and defective standard of North Germany! Were they not unanimous in their condemnation of Ernst Koerner's splendid picture, in which the daring artist represents a sunset in Alexandria as brilliantly as it is true to nature? And yet the latter bears the same relation to the gorgeous spectacle of Mirissa as the scant vegetation of Egypt does to the wanton exuberance of Ceylon. However what will not bloom along the Spree may not be found in India! Were not many of Edouard Hildebrand's color-effects pronounced "exaggerated," when "too weak" might have been more properly applied? But enchanting natural exhibitions like these must be seen to be appreciated.

XIV.

KOGALLA AND BORALU.

AMONG the more distant excursions I undertook from Belligam into the surrounding country, those to Kogalla and Boralu are recalled with greatest pleasure, and are of sufficient interest to deserve brief mention. Among the numerous extensive lagoons along the south-west coast of Ceylon which connect many of the rivers debouching on the sea between Colombo and Matura, *Kogalla-Wewa*, the "Rocky Lake," is distinguished by extraordinary size and picturesque beauty. This lagoon lies half way between Point de Galle and Belligam, and is of considerable extent, as numerous arms stretch in different directions. Its banks everywhere form densely-wooded hills, above which rise the crests of multitudes of cocoa-palms. Numbers of tiny islands, some of them bare rocks, and some covered with palm-grove or jungle, lend a peculiar charm to the diversified scenery, as do also the idyllic habitations of the Singhalese, which are scattered in groups and singly throughout the verdant thickets. The vegetation is of a crisp freshness that cannot be surpassed. It was a lovely Sunday morning (December 18th) when I took my departure from Belligam before sunrise, in order to reach Kogalla in good season. My hospitable friend from Point de Galle, Mr. Scott, whom I was to meet at Kogalla, had sent a servant with a light wagon and fleet pony to fetch me from Belligam; and as we drove swiftly through the primitive villages along the Galle road the indolent inhabitants were just rising from their palm couches and preparing for a morning bath. Directly the young sunbeams penetrated the dew-bespangled groves they became alive with sound and motion, and I enjoyed anew the delicious morning life of the tropics which had so often before enchanted me. My arrival at the place of appointment preceded the time agreed upon by a whole hour; I had, therefore, sufficient time for a leisurely ramble through the beautiful grove. With Mr. Scott came another German countryman, Herr Reimer, a native of Hamburg, at present engaged in mercantile business in India. He had been on a pleasure excursion to Bombay, and was on his way back to Singapore, when chance willed that he should favor us with his company the day before he set sail for that busy port. We drove a short distance farther through the palm gardens, and stopped at a hut on the bank of the Kogalla Lake. Here, a double canoe, that had been tastefully decorated by its Singhalese crew with garlands of flowers and a canopy of braided palm leaves, was waiting for us. These double boats, which are in great favor on the lagoons as well as on the larger rivers, are constructed of two hollow parallel logs, from sixteen to twenty feet long, with a space of five or six feet between them. Stout planks are fastened on them, and over these are laid boards. Right and left are the slender stems of young areca palms which support a canopy of pandanus mats. Leaves of the fan-palm are stretched curtain-wise between the supports. The benches, which are ranged along both sides of this floating arbor, offer a shady seat from which one may comfortably view the surrounding lake scenery. Six or eight powerful oarsmen squat in the hollow logs, either in front or in the rear of the platform.

The narrow arm of the lagoon from which we sailed opens into the more extensive basin through a gateway formed by three immense cliffs. These granite blocks are called the "Three Brothers" (*Tunamalaja*), and are the favorite resort for numerous large crocodiles. No swimmer would be allowed to pass unharmed between these hideous sentinels, who lie here all day long sunning themselves with widely-gaping jaws.

The lagoon is encircled by dense forests, beyond which rise smiling hills covered with palms. But the principal charm of the lagoon is its pretty little islands decked with cocoa-palms. The slender, gracefully-curved white stems incline in every direction, so that those nearest the shore are reflected entire in the waveless surface of the lake.

while those farther inland stand proudly upright with their feathered crests raised towards heaven. A perfect model of such a cocoa bouquet is the charming little Gan-Duva, which lies in the harbor of Belligam immediately in front of the rest-house.

We landed on a little cocoa island of this sort in Kogalla Lake, to pay a visit to the happy family living in the midst of the lovely palm bouquet. Three naked children, who had been frolicking among the rocks along the shore, at our approach ran screaming with terror towards their mother. The handsome young matron, with a fourth child in her arms, seemed also alarmed by the strange visitors, and hurried with her little ones into the bamboo hut. Her husband, who had been digging sweet potatoes in the garden, now appeared. The shapely, handsome fellow—he was entirely naked except the narrow strip of cloth around his loins—came forward, and after respectfully saluting us, asked whether we would like to refresh ourselves with some *curumba* (young cocoanuts). On our gratefully assenting he immediately climbed one of the tallest palms, and flung down half a dozen of the fine golden fruit known here as the "king's cocoanut." The cool, delicious water it contains is very like lemonade, and is wonderfully refreshing. Then he offered us some luscious bananas on a large caladium leaf, and conducted us into his garden, in which he cultivates a number of choice tropical plants. In answer to our query whether he could grow enough to supply the needs of his family for the entire year, he informed us that in addition to the products of his garden, he caught fish and crabs in the lake, and that he sold enough of these and of the fruits and vegetables he could not use, to buy all the rice and household articles required by his family—more he did not need, or want. Enviable family! In your little cocoa world you live as in a veritable paradise, and no covetous neighbor disturbs your happiness and peace!

We rowed farther out on the lake to a rock island, from whose dense shrubbery peered the white dagoba tower of a Buddhist temple. A flight of stone steps leads from the shore to the temple, on whose altar devout worshippers had scattered offerings of fragrant flowers. The rude wall-paintings, as well as the gigantic image of Buddha, are not different from those I saw in other Buddhist temples. In the rear of the temple are the habitations of the priests, picturesquely situated in the shade of a large Bo-tree, and affording a fine view of the lagoon; the red cliffs form natural terraces. A couple of tall kitool palms, as well as a handsome group of cocoa and areca palms, are as effective in the adornment of this charming picture as are the luxuriant vines of all sorts that festoon the crowns of several mighty cashew trees (*Anacardium*). It was intensely hot when at noon we rowed back to the chief's hut. The perfectly motionless water reflected the direct rays of the glowing sun like polished metal; we were therefore agreeably surprised to find the temperature in the dusky interior of the hut delightfully cool, and enjoyed the elaborate luncheon which had been prepared for us by Mr. Scott's servant with a keen relish. The meal over, and while my friends indulged in a siesta, I rowed across the lagoon to visit the two large Buddha temples on the opposite shore, and to gather some of the splendid orchids and spice lilies (*Marantaceæ*) growing there. I also enriched my sketchbook with several charming subjects, and had to pay for the pleasure with my blood, as multitudes of pestiferous leeches infest the grass along the shore.

No less attractive if not so extensive as Kogalla-Wewa, is another lagoon, Boralu-Wewa, or "Pebble Lake," which I visited several times. I am indebted for the pleasant days I spent there to the second head-man of Belligam, the excellent Arachy.

He owns a large tract of land in the immediate vicinity of the lagoon, that is planted partly with fruits of various kinds and partly with lemon grass, in the cultivation of which from thirty to forty laborers are employed. The road to Boralu traverses the luxuriant hill country, which stretches for many miles to the foot of the mountains.

The first natural curiosity encountered on this road is a mighty cocoa-palm, one mile from Belligam, whose stem is divided into three branches, each bearing a crown of foliage. This is an abnormity of rare occurrence. The second wonder is found a mile farther on, on the hither shore of the Polwatta River, beside a Buddha temple at the end of the bridge. It is a magnificent old banyan tree, fantastically garlanded with lianas of all sorts. On the further shore of the river, near Dena-Pitya (*i.e.*, cattle field), is another huge banyan, a very giant of his order, and one of the largest of these most remarkable trees in existence. The enormous crown, under which more than a hundred huts might find room and shade, is supported by multitudes of powerful stems, each one of which would deserve admiration were it a single tree. These huge trunks are nothing but the air-roots which have grown from the branches of the main stem. Between them hang numbers of smaller roots which have not yet reached the ground, and which elucidate the origin of the numerous supports. The densest shadow reigns beneath the leafy canopy through which no ray of light ever penetrates; and one can readily understand why the superstitious Buddhist approaches his sacred fig tree with timid reverence and awe.

A natural curiosity of quite a different order is to be found in the village of Dena-Pitya. It is a woman of perhaps fifty years, in whom the bones of the thighs are entirely wanting. The upper part of her body, which is well formed and fully developed, rests on the lower bones of the leg. This singular deformity is all the more curious from the fact that the woman has borne three well-formed children, who, like the mother, have only four toes on each foot. Unfortunately a closer investigation is not permitted.

If you follow the road eastward from Dena-Pitya for several miles you will arrive at the celebrated "gem pits," which, in the preceding century, were reputed to have been exceedingly productive. At present they seem to be exhausted, but a large diamond had been lately found that was sold for £400. This, of course, had attracted numbers of gem hunters to the deserted pits, and the day I visited them, from 160 to 180 laborers were busily washing and sifting gravel in the different excavations.

From Dena-Pitya the road to Boralu trends in a northeasterly direction, now through lovely palm-forest, now through luxuriant jungle, now across pale green paddy fields or marshy meadows, in which black buffaloes with their attendant herons wallow in the mud. Several miles farther on we come to the lagoon, whose entire shore is adorned with the most exuberant vegetation. Around it on every side rise densely-wooded hills. A small island, also clothed with verdant thicket, lies solitary and alone in the middle of the lagoon. But its greatest charm is the perfect solitude and absence of all human culture. Even the road which skirts its banks does not betray the presence of man, for it is quite hidden by the tall shrubbery.

The lagoon, as well as the adjacent region, is rich in animal life. As often as I visited it I found large green lizards from six to seven feet long sunning themselves on the shore, and once I was startled by an enormous snake (*Python molurus*) about twenty feet long. Unfortunately the monster slipped into the water before I could get a shot at him. Exciting sport is offered by the apes, whose grunts are heard on every side. I shot several fine examples of the yellow-brown "rilawa" (*Macacus sinicus*), and the large black wanderoo (*Presbytis cephalopterus*). But the most fruitful chase was after water-fowl, especially the different species of coot, herons, ibis, flamingoes, pelicans, etc. Large flocks of these birds at sundown fly across the lagoon to their nightly quarters. I once brought down half a dozen in a quarter of an hour. Numbers of smaller birds inhabit the thick brushwood along the shore, which is profusely adorned with splendid golden cassia flowers and the crimson blossoms of the melastoma.

Not far from the northern extremity of the lagoon, and separated from it by one or two wooded hills, lies the Arachy's woodland garden, a charming spot in which I spent four delightful days. The simple reed hut in which I lodged is entirely hidden by banana trees, and stands on the slope of a hill, from which there is a fine view of the verdant meadows, dark forests, and glimmering lagoons of the surrounding country; the distant background is formed by the blue mountains of the central highlands. Of the laborers' huts scattered throughout the forest there is nothing to be seen, and the delightful impression of absolute solitude is heightened by the unusually rich development of animal life. I shot numbers of beautiful birds, apes, flying foxes, lizards, etc., and once a large porcupine (*Hystrix leucura*) over three feet long.

Gorgeous butterflies and beetles are also numerous. The meadows in the vicinity of the lagoon are covered with gigantic specimens of the curious insectivorous pitcher-plant (*Nepenthes distillatoria*). The elegant pitchers, six inches long at the termination of the leaves, are covered with dainty lids, and frequently filled with captive insects. Brilliant *Ampelidæ* and lovely *Nectariniæ*, like the humming-birds which they strongly resemble, sport among the flowers in great numbers.

A ramble around the glittering lagoon will lead you through the most beautiful part of the woodland. In some places the vines which overrun the fallen trees form so impenetrable a barrier that it is utterly impossible to force your way through the vegetable chaos without the aid of an axe. Aristolochias, pepper-vines, bauhinias, and bignonias everywhere twist and twine among the branches in such a manner that only an occasional sunbeam penetrates the tangled mass. The trunks of the trees are covered with parasitic ferns and orchids. Often I sat for hours intent upon securing a copy of this forest picture for my sketch-book. Usually, however, my intentions were without result, my attempts futile. It was utterly impossible to adequately portray the bewildering loveliness of the scene. Nor was the photographic camera of any assistance. The verdant tangle was so dense, so intricate, that a photograph would have reproduced only a confused medley of stems, branches, foliage, etc.

On the slopes of the hills which encircle his garden the Arachy cultivates lemon grass, from which, by a simple process of distillation, is extracted the odorous lemon-oil, a highly-prized perfume. The lemon-like fragrance perfumes the whole neighborhood. The laborers employed in the distillery and in cultivating the banana plants, live in the tiny huts scattered throughout the grove; groups of slender cocoa and areca palms, as well as sturdy kitools and talipots, whose feathered crests tower above the lower trees, betray the hiding-places of these bamboo habitations. My visits to the latter, and friendly intercourse with their dusky occupants, made me almost envy the lot of this simple and contented nature-folk. They are pure Singhalese, with clear bronze complexions and delicate forms. The nimble boys were of great assistance to me in collecting plants and insects, while the graceful black-eyed girls decorated my little bullock cart with garlands of flowers.

When, late in the evening, the swift-footed zebu was harnessed, and the two-wheeled cart, in which there was scarcely room for me beside the Arachy, was set in motion, it was the special delight of these sprightly children to run after us. Frequently a swarm of twenty or thirty of the merry elves surrounded our cart, shouting and waving palm leaves. I could not sufficiently admire their perseverance and fleetness of motion.

When we entered the darkening grove, the boys would kindle torches and run in front of the cart to light the way. At an abrupt turn of the road we would occasionally be deluged with a shower of fragrant blossoms, a ripple of laughter in the dense shrubbery betraying the pranks of the mischievous dryads in hiding there. Among the latter was a niece of the Arachy's, whose perfect form might have served as a model for a sculptor, while the beauty of several of the lads rivalled even that of Ganymede.

One of the nimble fellows would occasionally swing himself to the pole of our swiftly-rolling cart, then leap dextrously over the zebu. With such performances the Boralu children would accompany us a long distance, then vanish one by one into the darkness of the night. And now, instead of the palm torches of our merry escort, myriads of fireflies and glow-worms would illumine the forest, while I and the Arachy, each busy with his own thoughts, drove swiftly toward the quiet rest-house of Belligam.

XV.

Matura and Dondera.

The most distant excursion I made during my sojourn in Belligam, was to the southern point of Ceylon, the long-celebrated Thunder Cape, Dondera Head. Near this point, but a few miles to the westward, is the city of Matura, situated on the banks of the Nilwella-ganga (blue sand river). The road from Belligam to Matura, which I traversed in three hours on the morning of the 18th of January, is a continuation of the beautiful palm avenue from Galle to Belligam, and abounds in the same picturesque and agreeably diversified scenery.

Matura, which is the most southerly of Ceylon's cities, was, during the reign of the Dutch, in the seventeenth century, a prosperous and important commercial station, and the principal port for the cinnamon trade of the South Province. The most imposing buildings in the city, as well as the considerable fort near the mouth of the river on the east bank, betray their Dutch origin. The noble stream is here about the width of the Elbe at Dresden, and is spanned by a handsome new iron suspension bridge. At the western end of the bridge, on the right bank of the river, is the ancient "star fort" of the Dutch, in whose angular casemates, at the invitation of several hospitable English officers, I took up my abode for three or four days. The three jolly bachelors had made themselves very comfortable in the low, many angled chambers of the ancient fortress, whose massive stone walls preserved the most delightful coolness. The walls were tastefully adorned, partly with wood-cuts from various illustrated newspapers, and partly with Singhalese weapons, curiosities, and skins of animals. Through the ancient Dutch gateway, above which the inscription, "Redoute van Eck" may still be seen, you enter a neat flower garden; luxuriant creepers and climbers decorate the embrasures in the walls and the draw-well in the centre of the garden. A pair of tame apes and a comical old pelican, as well as some small birds, furnish continual amusement.

A refreshing bath and an excellent English breakfast with my friendly hosts, which was keenly relished after the vegetarian diet of Belligam, so restored me that I was ready in a few hours after my arrival for an excursion to Dondera. This I undertook in a carriage, accompanied by the Chief Ilangakuhn, the most distinguished Singhalese on the island. He is the last male descendant of the illustrious race of ancient Kandyan kings, and has taken up his residence in Matura in a large, handsome, indeed, almost sumptuous palace, near the mouth of the river. He had called to see me at Belligam the week before, had presented me with several rare and beautiful birds, and invited me to visit him at Matura. His reception of me was as cordial as it was flattering. He would not allow any one but himself to drive me to Dondera. His equipage consisted of an elegant English phaeton, drawn by two splendid Australian horses; the fore-runner was a swift-footed Tamil in a silver-embroidered uniform and red turban.

The charming road from Matura to the five miles distant Dondera Head, runs in an easterly direction along the left bank of the Nilwella River, through the pettah, the picturesque "Black Town," which extends from the east side of the fort. The wooded hills between the river and the seashore, are adorned with flourishing gardens and attractive villas, the property of distinguished Singhalese and English Government officials. Farther on, the road skirts the seashore, and occasionally traverses a stretch of jungle or cocoa-grove. Here the latter has almost reached its eastern limit; for but a few miles farther are the first of the desolate and barren salt marshes, which extend along the east coast from Hambantotte to Batticaloa.

Dondera Head, or Thunder Cape, a considerable projection covered with groves of cocoa-palms, is visible for a long distance. It is the most southerly point of the island, and is situated in 5° 56′ N. latitude. For more than two thousand years the temples, which occupy this southern landmark, have been the resort of frequent pilgrimages, and are second in fame only to Adam's Peak. Thousands of pilgrims annually express their devotion for Dondera Head, whose temples have been dedicated alternately to Buddha and Vishnu, according to the faith of the predominant race, whether Singhalese or Malabar. Not longer than three hundred years ago, the principal temple was an edifice of the highest order of Indian architecture—so extensive and imposing, that from the sea it appeared like a considerable city with thousands of columns and statues, ornamented with gold and precious stones. In 1587 all this magnificence was destroyed or carried off by the Portuguese barbarians; but one may even yet obtain an idea of the former temple's enormous extent from the numerous broken columns which protrude from the ruins. In one corner of the latter is an immense dagoba, beside which are several colossal old Bo-trees.

The remains of a smaller temple are on the extreme point of the cape; they are octagonal pillars of red porphyry, rising solitary and deserted from the bare granite cliffs, encompassed by the surging billows that rage and foam around them. In the natural basins between the cliffs I collected at low tide a number of interesting sea creatures; lovely bits of coral are scattered everywhere. Westward from this isolated lookout, the glance roams along the cocoa-fringed strand to Matura; eastward to Tangalla; northward, dark forest masses intercept the view; while toward the south immeasurable space greets the roving eye. The tiny bark of fancy we send from here in full sail toward the south will meet with no know land this side of the pole; it would sail unhindered around the entire southern half of the globe, were it not for the stupendous ice masses of the antarctic regions, and reach land again only in the northern hemisphere, near Acapulco, Mexico. Occupied with thoughts like these I sat for a long time on this extreme point of Ceylon—also the most southerly point I had ever reached. I was roused from my nautical reverie by a company of Buddha priests that came to escort Ilaugakuhn and me to the flower-adorned temple. Afterwards we visited another cyclopean ruin in the adjacent grove, and returned to Matura late in the evening.

The following day (Jan. 19th) was occupied by a distant marine excursion in the eight-oared boat which Ilaugakuhn had placed at my disposal, and in which I sailed a considerable distance south of Dondera Head. It was glorious summer weather; the vigorous north-east monsoon blew so persistently against the large square sail, that two of the boatmen were obliged to sit on the outrigger to prevent the boat from capsizing. Our speed was almost equal to that of a swift steamer; I estimated it at about ten or twelve nautical miles an hour. The ease with which these narrow Singhalese canoes cut through the waves, or rather glide across their crests, was perfectly illustrated by our gallant craft. The farther we sailed from the island the more beautiful appeared the blue mountains of the highlands above the cocoa-forests of the coast—Adam's Peak as usual towering conspicuously above all the rest.

Swift as an arrow we sped across the foaming billows, and had reached a distance of perhaps forty or fifty miles south of Dondera Head when we saw a broad, smooth streak in the ocean which extended for miles in the direction of the monsoon, from north-east to south-west. This I at once decided to be a pelagic stream or current, one of those smooth, narrow water roads which are of frequent occurrence in the Mediterranean as well as in the larger oceans, and which owe their origin to the social amalgamation of extensive shoals of marine animals. When we drew nearer my surmise proved correct, and I was rewarded by an extraordinarily abundant and interesting catch. A dense mass of the most beautiful pelagic animals: medusæ, siphonophora, ctenophora and salpæ, sagitta and pteropods, besides countless numbers of larval worms, star-fish, crabs, mollusks, etc., swam about in the greatest confusion, and in a short time filled every vessel I had brought with me. I was only sorry I could not secure more of these zoological treasures (among them were many new and hitherto undescribed forms) to carry back with me to Europe. Richly laden with this wonderful catch, that promised to supply me with interesting work for the remainder of the year, I returned late in the afternoon to Matura. It was a beautiful souvenir of the fifth degree of north latitude. My Singhalese boatmen knew so well how to adapt the northeast monsoon to their use, that the speed of our outward voyage was almost equalled by our return to the island, where we landed at the mouth of the Nilwella-ganga. The view of the river from the sea is very picturesque, as a large rocky island lies like a sentinel directly in its mouth. Both shores are clothed with forest. The following day I rowed some distance up the river, and again admired the matchless exaberence of the primitive forest masses.

Returned to Belligam I was confronted by the most difficult task of any I had yet accomplished in Ceylon—that of bidding farewell to this enchanting region of the earth, in which I had spent six of the happiest as well as most interesting months of my life. Even yet the thought of that farewell weighs as heavily on my mind as if the parting was still before me. The familiar room which, during all this time, had served as work, living, and sleeping room, as laboratory, museum, and studio, in which I had collected a wealth of the most exquisite impressions, was empty and deserted. Under the giant teak tree in the garden, stood the heavily-laden bullock carts which were to carry my thirty chests of specimens to Point de Galle. In front of the gate waited the dusky inhabitants of the village, to whom for forty days I had been an object of constantly-increasing wonderment and curiosity. I had to take leave personally of all the more distinguished Belligamians, at their head the two chiefs who had treated me with unfailing courtesy. With a sorrowful mien good old Socrates for the last time brought me his choicest bananas, mangoes, ananas, and cashew nuts. For the last time Babua climbed my favorite palm to pluck for me its golden fruit. But the greatest trial of all was the farewell to my faithful Ganymede. The dear lad wept bitterly, and piteously besought me to take him to Europe. In vain I told him of the icy climate and gray skies of our dreary North—he clasped his arms around my knees and vowed that he was ready to follow me anywhere. I was almost compelled to force myself from his clinging arms, and when I waved a last adieu with my handkerchief to all the dear brown friends, I felt as if I were quitting Paradise. Beautiful Gem! Bella Gemma.

THE END.

The Cheapest and Best
Scouring Soap,
IN THE WORLD.
Price 10c. per Cake.

A GENUINE FILTER AT LAST, FOR 50 CTS.

No House should be without one. Also indispensable to Travelers. It is a genuine Filter, and will last for years. Price, 50 cents, mailed free. STODDARD LOCK CO., 104 Reade St., N. Y.

A new edition of Canon Farrar's great work,

EARLY DAYS OF CHRISTIANITY,

1 Vol., 12mo, cloth, gilt, - - - - - - - - - - $1.00
1 "   "   half calf. - - - - - - - - - , 2.50
This edition is printed from large, clear type, on good paper and very attractively bound. The half-calf edition will make a very handsome Christmas present for your Clergyman or Sunday School Teacher. The above work is also issued in 2 vols., in neat paper covers, as No. 50, Lovell's Library.
No. 50. Early Days of Christianity, by Canon Farrar, - Part I, .20
 "   "   "   "   "   "   "   - " II, .20

Recently Published:

Divorce, an original Novel, by Margaret Lee. 1 Vol. 12mo, neat
paper cover, - - - - - - - - - - .20
1 Vol., 12mo cloth, black and gold, - - - - - - - .50
A powerful American Novel, dealing with a subject of vital importance at the present day.

JOHN W. LOVELL CO., Publishers,
14 AND 16 VESEY STREET, NEW YORK.

STANDARD PUBLICATIONS.

Chas. Dickens' Complete Works, 15 Vols., 12mo, cloth, gilt, $22.50.
W. M. Thackeray's Complete Works, 11 Vols., 12mo, cloth, gilt, $16.50.

George Eliot's Complete Works, 8 Vols., 12mo, cloth, gilt, $10.00.
Plutarch's Lives of Illustrious Men, 3 Vols., 12mo. cloth, gilt, $4.50.

JOHN W. LOVELL CO., Publishers,
14 AND 16 VESEY STREET, NEW YORK.

STANDARD PUBLICATIONS.

Rollins' Ancient History, 4 Vols., 12mo, cloth, gilt, $6.00.
Charles Knight's Popular History of England, 8 Vols., 12mo, cloth, gilt top, $12.00.

Lovell's Series of Red Line Poets, 50 Volumes of all the best works of the world's great Poets, Tennyson, Shakespere, Milton, Meredith, Ingelow, Proctor, Scott, Byron, Dante, &c. $1.25 per volume.

JOHN W. LOVELL CO., Publishers,
14 AND 16 VESEY STREET, NEW YORK.

A ROMANCE,

By GEORGE WALKER.

No. 13 OF LOVELL'S LIBRARY.
PAPER COVERS, 20 CENTS.

"It possesses all the marked and prominent features which take fast hold upon the ordinary novel reader's fancy at once, and was therefore read by old and young with avidity, boys and girls smuggling it into their schools and homes, much to the dismay of prudent parents, who had already mastered its exciting contents in secret. It is full of a most intense kind of interest—love scenes, mysterious men and women, emissaries of the Inquisition, priests, bandits, outlaws, dark cells, subterranean passages, and lovely and unfortunate women, being found in every chapter."—*Albany Times.*

"A romance of the most dramatic character, replete with anecdote, adventure, and fine descriptive passage. For light reading, this is one of the most entertaining of books."—*The Dispatch, Pittsburgh.*

"If you read it in the night, it would be apt to make you back into bed, so that you might keep your eye on what was going on in your room until your head was safely covered by the bed clothes."—*The Elmira Advertiser.*

FOR SALE BY ALL NEWSDEALERS & BOOKSELLERS.

JOHN W. LOVELL CO., Publishers.
14 & 16 Vesey Street, N. Y.

[*January*, 1883.

JOHN W. LOVELL COMPANY'S
DESCRIPTIVE CATALOGUE OF
Standard and Miscellaneous Books

Alexander (Mrs.) Works by
The Wooing O't. By MRS. ALEXANDER. 1 vol., 16mo. Cloth extra, black and gold..................................50 cts.
Also in paper covers, in Lovell's Library, in two parts, each............15 cts.

The Admiral's Ward. By MRS. ALEXANDER. 1 vol., 16mo, cloth extra, black and gold....................................50 cts.
Also in paper covers, in Lovell's Library. *In press*....................20 cts

American Illustrated Pronouncing Dictionary of the English Language. Containing upwards of 25,000 words. Orthography, Pronunciation and Definitions, according to the best English and American Lexicographers. With an Appendix containing Abbreviations, Foreign Words and Phrases, etc. Illustrated with over 200 engravings, strongly bound in cloth.......................30 cts.

Andersen, (Hans Christian).
Fairy Tales. By HANS CHRISTIAN ANDERSEN. New plates, large clear type, handsomely printed and illustrated. 1 vol., 12mo, cloth, black and gold..$1 00

Anstey, (F.)
Vice-Versa, or, a Lesson to Fathers. By F. ANSTEY. 1 vol., 16mo, cloth extra, black and gold. ....50 cts.
Also in paper covers, Lovell's Library No. 30.........................20 cts.

Arabian Nights Entertainment.

The Thousand and One Nights. Translated from the Arabic. New plates, large clear type. 1 vol., 12mo., illustrated, cloth, black and gold...$1 00

Generations of wise fathers and mothers have thoroughly proved the high educational value of the ARABIAN NIGHTS *as a book of amusing stories for children. They stimulate young minds and create a taste and desire for reading at a time when almost all other forms of literature would be irksome and uninstructive. Hardly any one that does not date the first real impulse given to his intellectual faculties back to his first acquaintance with* SINBAD THE SAILOR, ALADDIN AND HIS WONDERFUL LAMP, *and the* HISTORY OF THE ENCHANTED HORSE. *Beside the infinite enjoyment that is afforded the child, a familiarity with the characteristic features of Oriental literature is acquired which is of permanent value in the education of after years.*

Aytoun (William Edmondstone).

Lays of the Scottish Cavaliers and other Poems. By WILLIAM EDMONDSTONE AYTOUN, Professor of Rhetoric and English Literature in the University of Edinburgh. Red Line Edition. 1 vol., 12mo. Cloth, gilt, gilt edges. $1 25.

Professor Aytoun has selected his themes from striking incidents and stirring scenes in mediæval Scotch history, and thrown over them the light of an imagination at once picturesque and powerful. Finer ballads than these are not to be found in the English language, if in any. Full of the true fire, they now stir and swell with the stirring ring of the trumpet, now sink in cadences sad and wild as a Highland dirge. We feel, when we read these lays, that we are dealing not with shadows, but with living men. The poems which form part of the volume with the Lays are gems which, while they add to the poet's reputation for versatility, add also to his fame; what they lack of the heroic element which makes the ballads so fascinating, they make up in a charm wholly their author's and their own.

Besant (Walter) and James Rice.

They Were Married. By WALTER BESANT and JAMES RICE. 16mo, paper covers, Lovell's Library No. 18.........................10 cts.

Björnson (Björnstjerne).

The Happy Boy and Arne. Tales of Norwegian Country Life. Two vols. in one. 16mo, cloth extra, black and gold..........50 cts.
Also, published separately in Lovell's Library—
No. 3. The Happy Boy. Paper cover.................................10 cts.
No. 4. Arne. Paper covers..10 cts.

Balzac (Honoré de).

The Vendetta; tales of Love and Passion. By HONORÉ DE BALZAC. 1 vol., 16mo, cloth, black and gold.....................50 cts.
Also, in paper covers, in Lovell's Library..........................20 cts.

Black (William).

A Princess of Thule. By WM. BLACK. 1 vol., 16mo, cloth extra, black and gold...50 cts.
Also, in paper covers, Lovell's Library No. 48......................20 cts.

An Adventure in Thule and Marriage of Moira Fergus. By WM. BLACK. Paper covers, Lovell's Library No. 40............10 cts.

Broughton (Rhoda).
Second Thoughts. By RHODA BROUGHTON, 1 vol., 16mo, cloth, black and gold...50 cts.
Also, in paper covers, Lovell's Library No. 23.................20 cts.

Bulwer's Novels.
One-volume Edition. Containing a selection of the best novels of Sir EDWARD BULWER (Lord Lytton), as follows:—

The Last Days of Pompeii. | Eugene Aram.
Ernest Maltravers. | Pelham.
Alice. | Zanoni.
Godolphin.
1 vol., 8vo., cloth, black and gold... ....$2 00
Also see LYTTON, LORD.

Bunyan (John).
The Pilgrim's Progress from this World to that which is to come, delivered under the similitude of a dream. By JOHN BUNYAN. 1 vol., 12mo, illustrated, cloth, black and gold................$1 00

Burns (Robert).
The complete Poetical Works of ROBERT BURNS, to which is added his correspondence. Large, clear type, new plates. Red Line Edition. 1 vol., 12mo, handsomely bound in cloth, gilt, gilt edges..$1 25

Burns is by far the greatest poet that ever sprung from the bosom of the people. He was born a poet, if ever man was, and his rank, as Byron said, " is the first in his art." He possessed all the essentials of a poet's great humor, great powers of description, great discrimination of character, and great pathos. His conceptions are all original, his thoughts new, and his style unborrowed. His language is familiar, yet dignified, careless, yet concise ; he sheds a redeeming light on all he touches, and whatever he glances at rises into life and beauty. His variety is equal to his originality. It is as infinite as his power in expression, and the result of these combined faculties has been such verse as the world will, in all liklihood, never see again. Long after more pretentious rhyme writers have been forgotten, the poet of the fields and of the cotter's cabin will be quoted wherever the language he became illustrious in is known.

Byron, Lord.
The complete Poetical Works of LORD BYRON, printed in clear type on good paper. Red Line Edition. 1 vol., 12mo, illustrated, cloth gilt, gilt edges...$1 25

" In the United States, Byron will always occupy a high place as the poet of the passions, and it is said, that after Shakespeare he is the most popular of the English poets. The least successful of Byron's productions, notwithstanding the admirable passages with which they abound, are his tragedies ; the work that gives us the highest notion of his genius, power and versatility is his DON JUAN. *The Don is at times free and almost obscene, and the whole tendency of the poem may be considered immoral; but there are scattered throughout it the most exquisite pieces of writing and feeling—inimitable blendings of wit, humor, raillery and pathos, and by far the finest verses Byron ever wrote. He may be said to have created this manner; for the Bernesco style of the Italians, to which it has been compared, is not like it."—Life and Literary Labors of* LORD BYRON.

Californians and Mormons.
Sketches of American Life, Manners and Institutions. By
A. F. D. DE RUPERT. 1 vol., 12mo, cloth, black and gold..........$1 00

Campbell (Thomas).
The Poetical Works of THOMAS CAMPBELL, with Notes and Biographical Sketch. Printed in clear type, on good paper. Red Line Edition.
1 vol., 12mo, illustrated, cloth, gilt, gilt edges......................$1 25

I do not think I overrate the merits of the "Pleasures of Hope," whether taking it in its parts, or as a whole, in preferring it to any didactic poem in the English language. No poet at such an age ever produced such an exquisite specimen of poetical mastery; that is, of fine conception and of high art combined. Sentiments tender, energetic, impassioned, eloquent, majestic, are conveyed to the reader in the tones of a music forever varied, sinking or swelling like the harmonies of an Æolian lyre, yet ever delightful; and these are illustrated by pictures from romance, history, or domestic life, replete with power and beauty.—MOIR'S *Lectures on Poetry.*

"Cavendish."
Card Essays, Clay's Decisions and Card-Table-Talk. By "CAVENDISH," 1 vol., 16mo, cloth, gilt.................75 cts.

The Laws and Principles of Whist, carefully revised, with diagram cards, printed in two colors; to which is added Card Essays, Clay's Decisions and Card-Table Talk, with portrait of "CAVENDISH."
1 vol., 16mo, cloth, black and gold $1 50

Chaucer (Geoffrey).
The Poetical Works of GEOFFREY CHAUCER, with Memoir. Printed in clear type, on good paper. Red Line Edition. 1 vol., 12mo. Illustrated, cloth, gilt, gilt edges.. .... $1 25

Chaucer has well been called the father of English poetry. In elocution and eloquence, in grace and harmony of versification, he surpassed all his predecessors, and for the first time in English literature created verse which was true poetry, not mere doggrel rhyme. His genius was universal, and the themes he exercised it in, consequently, of boundless variety. He painted familiar manners with the touch of a master, which to this day impresses the reader of the pages penned five centuries ago with the haunting idea that the poet's characters are alive and moving in a pageant before him. His humor was as natural and unforced as his pathos was deep, his sentiment pure, and his passion fiery and genuine. It was Coleridge who said of Chaucer, "I take unceasing delight in him. His manly cheerfulness is especially delicious to me in my old age. How exquisitely tender he is, yet how perfectly free from the least touch of sickly melancholy or morbid drooping." The verdict of Coleridge has been the verdict of the whole reading world.

Child's History of England.
Child's History of England. By CHARLES DICKENS. A New Edition for the use of Schools. With numerous illustrations. Printed from large type, illustrated, 1 vol., 12mo...................................$1 00

Charles Dickens wrote the Child's History of England for his own children, because as he himself says, he could find nothing in the whole line of English histories just suitable for them; at a time when they were beginning to read with interest and profit, but not sufficiently advanced to take up the great standard authors. It was a labor of love, and had been well appreciated by the multitudes of young people who have gained their first knowledge of history from this delightful little volume. It is written in the most pure and simple language, and has for young readers all the picturesque and vivid interest that one of the author's novels possesses for the older ones. All the great characters of English history become as familiar, and produce as permanent impressions, as the heroes of the Arabian Nights and of the other favorite books of childhood. It is not only indispensable in every household where any care at all is bestowed upon the education of children, but is also one of the best brief and compendious histories of England for all classes of readers.

Also see DICKENS (CHARLES).

Children of the Abbey.
A Tale. By REGINA MARIA ROCHE. 1 vol., 12mo, illustrated, cloth, gilt..$1 00

Of all the once popular novels of this once famous novelist, the "Children of the Abbey" alone remains. From the time of its first republication in this country it has retained its place in popular favor. No better example of the novel of our grandfathers could be found, and few more interesting ones are written in these days of the grandchildren.

Coleridge (Samuel Taylor).
The Poetical Works of SAMUEL TAYLOR COLERIDGE. With an introduction and Memoir. Red Line Edition. 1 vol., 12mo, cloth, gilt-edges...$1 25

Of all the illustrious English men of letters, Coleridge, with his spacious intellect, his subtle and comprehensive intelligence, holds rank with the first. As a poet he will live with the language. On his incomparable "Genevieve" he has lavished all the melting graces of poetry and chivalry; in his "Ancient Mariner" he has sailed, and in his "Christabel" flown to the very limits of invention and belief; and in his chant of "Fire, Famine and Slaughter" he has revived the startling strains of the furies, and given us a song worthy the prime agents of perdition.

Collins (Wilkie).
The Moonstone. By WILKIE COLLINS. 1 vol., 16mo, cloth, black and gold ....50 cts.
Also, in two volumes, Nos. 8 and 9. Lovell's Library, each............10 cts.
The New Magdalen. By WILKIE COLLINS. 1 vol., 16mo, cloth, black and gold..50 cts.
Also, in paper covers, Lovell's Library No. 24..................20 cts.

Cooper (J. Fenimore).
The Last of the Mohicans: A Narrative of 1757. By J. FENIMORE COOPER. Printed from large, clear type. 1 vol., 12mo, cloth, black and gold $1 00
Also in paper covers, Lovell's Library No. 26.....................20 cts.
The Spy. By J. FENIMORE COOPER. 16mo, paper covers, Lovell's Library, No. 53..20 cts.

Cowper (William).
The complete Poetical Works of WILLIAM COWPER. Printed from new plates, large, clear type, handsomely illustrated. Red Line Edition. 1 vol., 12mo, cloth, black and gold, gilt edges.............$1 25

Cowper was the poet of well educated and well principled England. His muse was as pure as his style, and his life conformed to both. His "Task" is a poem of such infinite variety that it seems to include all possible subjects. It contains pictures of domestic comfort and social refinement which can only be forgotten with the language itself.

Crabbe (George).
The Poetical Works of GEORGE CRABBE. Red Line Edition. 1 vol., 12mo, illustrated, cloth, gilt, gilt edges............................$1 25

Dr. Johnson, to whom Crabbe's first poem, "The Village," was submitted, pronounced it "original, vigorous and elegant." The public endorsed the great lexicographer's opinion, and Crabbe deserved it. His genius was essentially analytic and humane. He had a mortal hatred of wrong, and was never so active as when laying it bare to the world.

Dante Alighieri.
The Vision of Hell, Purgatory, and Paradise, of DANTE ALIGHIERI. Translated by the Rev. Henry Francis Cary, A. M. With the life of Dante and Chronological View of his age. Red Line Edition. 1 vol., 12mo, illustrated, cloth, gilt, gilt edges.................... $1 25

Of all the translations of Dante, Cary's has been conceded the most successful. It is executed with perfect fidelity and admirable skill. It would be impossible to transfer the lines of the great Italian poet into our language with any closer preservation of their beauties of rhythm and meaning than Mr. Cary has succeeded in accomplishing.

Detlef (Carl).
Irene; or, the Lonely Manor. By CARL DETLEF. 1 vol., 16mo, cloth, black and gold...50 cts
Also, in paper covers, in Lovell's Library, No. 29..................20 cts.

De Quincy (Thomas).
The Spanish Nun. By THOMAS DE QUINCY. 16mo, paper covers, Lovell's Library, No. 20..................................10 cts.

Dickens-Collins Xmas Stories.
No Thoroughfare and Two Idle Apprentices. By CHARLES DICKENS and WILKIE COLLINS. 1 vol., 12mo, cloth, black and gold, $1 00

Dickens (Charles).
CHARLES DICKENS' COMPLETE WORKS. Lovell's Popular Illustrated Edition. Printed from entirely new electrotype plates, large clear type, with over 150 illustrations by Phiz, Barnard, Green, etc., etc.

I. Pickwick Papers.
II. David Copperfield.
III. Martin Chuzzlewit.
IV. Nicholas Nickleby.
V. Bleak House.
VI. Little Dorrit.
VII. Dombey and Son.
VIII. Our Mutual Friend.
IX. Oliver Twist, Pictures from Italy, and American Notes.
X. Old Curiosity Shop and Hard Times.
XI. Tale of Two Cities and Sketches by Boz.
XII. Barnaby Rudge and Mystery of Edwin Drood.

Dickens (Charles)—Continued.

XIII. **Great Expectations, Uncommercial Traveller,** and **Miscellaneous.**
XIV. **Christmas Stories** and **Reprinted Pieces.**
XV. **Child's History of England** and **Miscellaneous.**
15 vols., 12mo, cloth, gilt..$22 50
15 vols., 12mo, half Russia... 33 00
15 vols., 12mo, half calf.. 45 00
Also published separately.

Child's History of England. By Charles Dickens. 1 vol., 12mo, cloth, black and gold..$1 00
Oliver Twist. By Charles Dickens. 1 vol., 12mo, cloth, black and gold..$1 00
Also, in paper covers, Lovell's Library No. 10............................20 cts.
A Tale of Two Cities. By Charles Dickens. 1 vol., 12mo, cloth, black and gold..$1 00
Also in paper covers, Lovell's Library No. 38...........................20 cts.

Dictionary of the Bible.
By Edward Robinson, D.D., with a history of the Bible, by William Smith, LL.D. 1 vol., 12mo, cloth, gilt........................$1 25

Don Quixote de la Mancha.
Translated from the Spanish of Miguel de Cervantes Saavedra. By Charles Jarvis. Carefully revised and corrected. Printed from new plates, large clear type, illustrated. 1 vol., 12mo, cloth, gilt, $1 00

Doré Gallery.
The Doré Gallery of Bible Stories, illustrating the principal events in the Old and New Testaments, with descriptive Text by Josephine Pollard. 1 large 4to volume, magnificently illustrated by Gustave Doré. Cloth, gilt..$3 00

Dryden (John).
The Poetical Works of John Dryden. Red Line Edition.
1 vol., 12mo, illustrated, cloth, gilt, gilt edges.........................$1 25
To read him is as bracing as a northwest wind. He blows the mind clear. In ripeness and bluff heartiness of expression he takes rank with the best. . To be among the first in any kind of writing, as Dryden certainly was, is to be one of a very small company.—John Russell Lowell.

Eliot (George), Works of
The Complete Works of George Eliot, beautifully printed from large, clear type, on good paper, and handsomely bound in cloth.
8 vols., 12mo, cloth, black and gold.............................$10 00
8 vols.,   "   on better paper, cloth, gilt top..................... 12 00
8 vols.,   "   "   half calf... 24 00

I. **Middlemarch.**
II. **Daniel Deronda.**
III. **Romola.**
IV. **Felix Holt.**
VIII. **The Spanish Gypsy,** Theophrastus Such.
V. **Romola.**
VI. **The Mill on the Floss.**
VII. **Scenes from Clerical Life** and **Silas Marner.**
Jubal and other Poems, and

Eliot (George).—CONTINUED.

Also published separately.
Adam Bede. By GEORGE ELIOT. 1 vol., 12mo, cloth, black
and gold..$1 00
Also in paper covers, in two parts, Lovell's Library No. 56, each........15 cts.

English Men of Letters.

English Men of Letters, edited by JOHN MORLEY. A series of Brief Biographies by the most eminent literary men of the day. 5 vols., 12mo. Printed from fine clear type, on good paper, handsomely bound in cloth, gilt...$3 75
Any volume sold separately, bound in cloth, gilt ....75 cts.

Vol. I. contains
Burns, by Principal Shairp.
Byron, by Professor Nichol.
Milton, by Mark Pattison.
Shelley, by J. A. Symonds.

Vol. II. contains
Chaucer, by Prof. A. W. Ward.
Cowper, by Goldwin Smith.
Pope, by Leslie Stephen.
Southey, by Prof. Dowden.

Vol. III. contains
Bunyan, by J. A. Froude.
Spenser, by the Dean of St. Paul's.
Locke, by Thomas Fowler.
Wordsworth, by F. Myers.

Vol. IV. contains
Burke, by John Morley.
Gibbon, by J. C. Morison.
Hume, by Prof. Huxley.
Johnson, by Leslie Stephen.

Volume V. contains
Defoe, by William Minto.
Goldsmith, by William Black.
Scott, by R. H. Hutton.
Thackeray, by Anthony Trollope.

Each Biography is also issued separately, in neat paper cover, price, including postage, 10 cents, viz.:—

Bunyan, by J. A. Froude.
Burke, by John Morley.
Burns, by Principal Shairp.
Byron, by Professor Nichol.
Chaucer, by Prof. A. W. Ward.
Cowper, by Goldwin Smith.
Defoe, by William Minto.
Gibbon, by J. C. Morison.
Goldsmith, by William Black.
Hume, by Professor Huxley.
Johnson, by Leslie Stephen.

Locke, by Thomas Fowler.
Milton, by Mark Pattison.
Pope, by Leslie Stephen.
Scott, by R. H. Hutton.
Shelley, by J. Symonds.
Southey, by Prof. Dowden.
Spenser, by the Dean of St. Paul's.
Thackeray, by Anthony Trollope.
Wordsworth, by F. Myers.

Farrar (F. W., D.D.) Works of

Seekers after God. By F. W. FARRAR, D.D. 1 vol., 16mo, cloth, black and gold...50 cts.
Also in paper covers, Lovell's Library No. 19............................20 cts.
Early Days of Christianity. By F. W. FARRAR, D.D. 1 vol., 12mo, cloth, gilt...$1 00
Also in paper covers, Lovell's Library, No. 50, in two parts, each........20 cts.

Favorite Pocket Dictionary of the English Language.
Based on the labors and principles of the latest and best American and English authorities. 1 vol., 16mo, 320 pages, cloth.........25 cts.

Favorite Poems.
Selections from the writings of the best Poets, with many poems by American authors. Red Line Edition. 1 vol., 12mo, cloth, gilt, gilt edges..$1 25

The most popular poems in the language have a place in this volume. Selected and edited with great care, they form a collection such as has never before been presented to the public, and one which is almost indispensable wherever the refined love for literature in its highest and most refined form exists.

Feuillet (Octave).
Marriage in High Life. By OCTAVE FEUILLET, translated by OLIVE LOGAN. 1 vol., 16mo, cloth, black and gold.............50 cts.
Also in paper covers, Lovell's Library No. 41.....................20 cts.

Frankenstein;
Or, the Modern Prometheus. By MARY WOLLSTONECRAFT SHELLEY. 1 vol., 16mo, cloth, black and gold....................50 cts.
Also in paper covers, 12mo, 177 pages, Lovell's Library No. 5.........10 cts.

Sir Walter Scott has said:

"Frankstein" has passages which appal the mind and make the flesh creep."

While Thornton Hunt, speaking of Mrs. Shelley, says:

"Her command of History and her imaginative power, are shown in such a book as, "Valperga;" but the daring originality of her mind comes out most distinctly in her earliest published work, 'Frankenstein.'

George (Henry).
Progress and Poverty. By HENRY GEORGE. 16mo, paper covers, Lovell's Library No. 52....................................20 cts.

Let us say, at the outset, that this is not a work to be brushed aside with lofty indifference or cool disdain. It is not the production of a visionary or a sciolist, of a meagerly equipped or ill-regulated mind. The writer has brought to his undertaking a comprehensive knowledge of the data and principles of science, and his skill in exposition and illustration attests a broad acquaintance with history and literature. Few books have, in recent years, proceeded from any American pen which have more plainly borne the marks of wide learning and strenuous thought, or which have brought to the expounding of a serious theme a happier faculty of elucidation.—New York Sun.

Gibbon (Charles).
The Golden Shaft. By CHAS. GIBBON. 1 vol., 16mo, cloth, black and gold..50 cts.
Also, in paper covers, in Lovell's Library, No. 57..................20 cts.

Goldsmith (Oliver).

The Poetical Works of OLIVER GOLDSMITH. Red Line Edition.
1 vol., 12mo, illustrated, cloth, gilt, gilt edges $1 25

Vicar of Wakefield. By OLIVER GOLDSMITH. Paper covers,
Lovell's Library, No. 51 .... 10 cts.
Also included, in 1 vol., cloth, 12mo, with Paul and Virginia and Rasselas,$1 00

Goldsmith, both in prose and verse, is one of the most delightful writers in the language. His verse flows like a limped stream. His Traveller is one of the most finished and noble poems ever written. His Deserted Village is a masterpiece, full of an accuracy of nature, in one of its sweetest phases, and a profound pathos inexpressibly touching and powerful.

Grant (James).

The Secret Dispatch. By JAMES GRANT. 1 vol., 16mo,
cloth, black and gold .... 50 cts.
Also in paper covers, Lovell's Library No. 49 .... 20 cts.

Grimm Brothers.

Grimm's Popular Tales. Collected by the BROTHERS GRIMM.
Printed from new plates, large, clear type, handsomely illustrated. 1 vol.,
12mo, cloth, black and gold $1 00

Gulliver's Travels and Baron Munchausen.

Gulliver's Travels. By DEAN SWIFT, to which is added **The Travels and Surprising Adventures of Baron Munchausen.** 2 vols. in one, 12mo. Illustrated, cloth, black and gold $1 00

See also SWIFT (DEAN).

Halevy (Ludovic).

L'Abbé Constantine. By LUDOVIC HALEVY. 1 vol., 16mo,
cloth, black and gold .... 50 cts.
Also in paper covers, Lovell's Library, No. 15 .... 20 cts.

Hatton (Joseph).

Clytie. A Novel. By JOSEPH HATTON. 1 vol., 12mo,
Lovell's Standard Library, cloth, black and gold $1 00
Also in Lovell's popular library, 1 vol., 16mo, cloth, extra black and gold.50 cts.
Also in paper covers. Lovell's Library, No. 7 .... 20 cts.

Hardy (Thomas).

Two on a Tower. By THOMAS HARDY. 1 vol., 16mo, cloth,
black and gold .... 50 cts.
Also, in paper covers, Lovell's Library, No. 43 .... 20 cts.

Hemans (Mrs. Felicia).

The Poetical Works of MRS. FELICIA HEMANS, edited with a critical Memoir by WILLIAM MICHAEL ROSSETTI. Illustrated by THOMAS SECOMBE. Printed from new plates, large clear type. Red Line Edition. 1 vol., 12mo. Illustrated, cloth, gilt, gilt edges $1 25

Mrs. Hemans has been called the most popular of female poets. Her genius was of the domestic order, and its eminations found the safest of all abiding places, that of the family and the fireside. She shows high sentiment and heoric feeling now and then, but her affections are with the gentle, the meek and the wounded in spirit. She is the authoress of many a plaintive and mournful strain, and her poetry throughout is intensely feminine. " Her best songs," as Allan Cunningham wrote, " have been rightly named of the affections."

Henley (Leonard).
Life of Washington. By LEONARD HENLEY. 1 vol. 16mo, cloth, black and gold... 50 cts.
Also in paper covers, Lovell's Library, No. 26... ....20 cts.

Herbert (George).
The works of GEORGE HERBERT in prose and verse, edited from the latest editions, with Memoir, explanatory notes, &c. Printed from new plates, large clear type, handsomely illustrated. Red Line Edition. 1 vol., 12mo, cloth, gilt, gilt edges..................................$1 25

The poems of George Herbert have stood the crucial test of two centuries of criticisms and come out pure gold. With their intense devotional feeling, they combine a quaint sweetness of expression and an earnest fluency of diction which lend them a charm peculiarly their own. His homlier poems, those on which the ingenuity of his cultivated mind was not lavished, but which were thrown off as the spontaneous productions of his unconventional muse. A model of a man and a clergyman, Herbert may almost be held up as a model of a poet too.

Homer.
The Odyssey of Homer. Translated by ALEXANDER POPE, with notes and introduction by the Rev. T. A. BUCKLEY, M.A., F.S.A. Red Line Edition. With Flaxman's Designs. 1 vol, 12mo, cloth, black and gold, gilt edges........... ....$1 25

The Iliad of Homer. Translated by ALEXANDER POPE, with notes and introduction by the Rev. T. A. BUCKLEY, M.A., F.S.A. Red Line Edition. With Flaxman's Designs. 1 vol., 12mo, cloth, black and gold, gilt edges...$1 25

Pope's translation of the Iliad was unquestionably the greatest literary labor ever executed. Dr. Johnson pronounced it the noblest version of poetry the world had ever seen, and called it a treasure of poetical elegance. It is in fact a marvelous work for purity of language and grace of style. There have been more faithful translations of Homer in the literal sense, but none which approached that of Pope in literary value.

Hood (Thomas).
The choice works of THOMAS HOOD, in Prose and Verse, including the cream of the Comic Annuals, with Life of the Author. Portrait and over 200 illustrations. 1 vol., 12mo, 780 pp., cloth............$2 00
Cheaper edition, 1 vol., 12mo, cloth, black and gold................... 1 00
The Poetical Works of THOMAS HOOD. Red Line Edition. 1 vol., 12mo, illustrated, cloth, gilt, gilt edges...$1 25

Hood's verse, whether serious or comic, is ever pregnant with materials for thoughts. Like every author distinguished for true comic humor, there is a deep vein of melancholy pathos running through his mirth. The same genius that created the Lost Boy gave birth to the Song of the Shirt, the Bridge of Sighs, and the Dream of Eugene Aram. While his lighter works bristle with wit and fine sarcasm, his serious ones are pregnant with such tenderness and such sense of nature, animate and inanimate, as few poets have ever peered.

Houdin (Robert).

The Tricks of the Greeks Unveiled; or, The Art of Winning at every Game. By ROBERT HOUDIN. Translated by M. I. Smithson. 1 vol., 16mo, cloth, black and gold...................................50 cts.
Also in paper covers, Lovell's Library No. 14.................. ....20 cts.

Ingelow (Jean).

The complete Poetical Works of JEAN INGELOW. Printed in clear type, on good paper. Red Line Edition. 1 vol., 12mo. Illustrated, cloth, gilt, gilt edges.. 1 25

The world has seen few sweeter singers than Jean Ingelow. Her poetical works have obtained a circulation and a popularity equally deserved. Her love of nature has found vent in simple lays which have stolen their ways to numberless hearts, while her poetic instinct has evinced itself in works of a high order of picturesqueness and art.

Ivanhoe.

By SIR WALTER SCOTT, Bart. From the last Edinburgh edition, with the author's final notes and corrections. 1 vol. 12mo. Illustrated cloth, gilt....... . ...1 00

Ivanhoe was given to the world in 1820, and within the year had been translated into most European languages. "Scott's bosom," says Prescott, "warmed with a sympathetic glow for the age of chivalry. No one can form an idea of the people who moved in it, of Richard Cœur de Lion and his brave paladins, that has not read Ivanhoe."

James (G. P. R.)

One-Volume Edition. Containing a selection of the best novels of this popular writer:—

One in a Thousand.	Philip Augustus.
Richelieu.	The Gypsy.
The Robbers.	The Ancient Régime.

The Gentleman of the Old School.
1 vol., 8vo, cloth, black and gold...$2 50

Jay (Harriett).

The Dark Colleen. By HARRIETT JAY. 1 vol., 16mo, cloth, extra black and gold...50 cts.
Also in paper covers, Lovell's Library No. 17.... ....20 cts.

Junius's Letters.

The Letters of Junius. WOODFALL'S edition. From the latest London edition. 1 vol. 12mo, cloth, black and gold..................$1 25

These letters of that mysterious genius Junius, whose identity is not known to this day, are reprinted from the edition issued by his own publisher, Woodfall. The classic purity of their language, the force and perspicuity of their arguments, the keen severity of their reproach, and the extensive information they evince, place these celebrated epistles in the first rank of English literature.

DISCRIPTIVE CATALOGUE. 13

Keats (John).
The Poetical Works of John Keats. Red Line Edition. 1 vol., 12mo. Illustrated, cloth, gilt edges......................... $1 25

In his Endymion Keats created a work which the critics have not done disputing over yet, but which the reading public acknowledges to be one of the most startling, novel, and fantastically beautiful epics which the muse of any modern mortal ever formed a conception of. Two works in which Keats is seen to his best advantage are his Lamia and Isabella. These, as well as his minor poems, are all included in the above edition.

Kingsley (Charles).
The Hermits. By CHAS. KINGSLEY. 1 vol. 16mo, cloth, black and gold..50 cts.
Also in paper covers, Lovell's Library No. 39........................20 cts.
Hypatia. By CHAS. KINGSLEY. 1 vol., 16mo, cloth, black and gold..50 cts.
Also in paper covers, Lovell's Library, in two parts, each..........15 cts

Knight (Charles).
Popular History of England, from the landing of Julius Cæsar to the death of Prince Albert. By CHARLES KNIGHT. Library Edition. 8 vols., 12mo. 160 illustrations, cloth, gilt top....... $12 00
The same, popular edition, 4 vols., 12mo. 32 illustrations, cloth, gilt.... $6 00

Knight's History of England has taken its place among the standard chronicles of the world. The critics pronounced the author, in consideration of his valuable work "one of the first literary benefactors of the age." The style is easy and graceful, and free from all the ponderousness and dryness of description which render so many histories unreadable.

Lamb (Charles).
The Complete Works, in Prose and Verse, of CHARLES LAMB, from the original edition, with the cancelled passages restored, and many pieces now first collected. Edited and prefaced by A. H. SHEPHERD. 1 vol., 12mo. Illustrated, 790 pp., cloth, extra gilt.... .... $2 00

Language and Poetry of Flowers.
Language and Poetry of Flowers. Selected from the best authors. Red Line Edition. 1 vol., 12mo. Illustrated, cloth, gilt, gilt edges..$1 25

Last Days of Pompeii.
See LORD LYTTON.

Last of the Mohicans.
See COOPER (J. FENIMORE).

Lee (Margaret).
Divorce. By MARGARET LEE. 1 vol., 16mo. cloth, black and gold..50 cts.
Also in paper Covers, Lovell's Library, No. 25..................20 cts.

Life and Letters of Lord Macaulay.

By his nephew GEORGE OTTO TREVELYAN, M.P. Two volumes in one. 1 vol., 12mo., cloth, gilt $1 25

The personality of Macaulay is marked in his written life as clearly as he ever marked that of any of his historic heroes. The letters and papers, the fragments of the great chronicler's work thus rescued from oblivion, are a mine of interest. The reader to whom Macaulay the litterateur has become familiar through his own productions, will never know Macaulay the man until he learns him through the medium of his nephew's pen picture.

Longfellow (H. W.) Works

Hyperion. A Romance. By H. W. Longfellow. 1 vol., 16mo, cloth, gilt.... .... 50 cts.
Also in paper covers, Lovell's Library, No. 1 .... 20 cts.

Outre-Mer. A Pilgrimage beyond the Sea. By H. W. LONGFELLOW. 1 vol., 16mo, cloth, gilt .... 50 cts.
Also in paper covers, Lovell's Library, No. 2 .... 20 cts.

Lovell's Red Line Poets.

Lovell's Red Line Edition of the Poets. Without doubt the finest and most complete edition of the poets ever issued in this country, at a low price. In 12mo volumes, illustrated, handsomely bound in cloth, black and gold, gilt edges $1 25

Arnold.	Goldsmith.	Pope.
Aytoun.	Hemans.	Procter.
Burns.	Hood.	Religious Poems.
Byron.	Herbert.	Schiller.
Browning.	Iliad.	Scott.
Chaucer.	Ingelow.	Shakspeare.
Campbell.	Keats.	Shelley.
Cowper.	Kirke White.	Spenser.
Crabbe.	Lucile.	Taylor's Philip van
Coleridge.	Milton.	Artevald.
Dante.	Moore.	Tennyson.
Dryden.	Macaulay.	Thomson.
Eliot.	Meredith.	Tupper.
Eliza Cook.	Ossian.	Virgil.
Favorite Poems.	Odyssey	White, Kirke.
Goethe.	Poe.	Willis.
Goethe's Faust.	Poetry of Flowers.	Wordsworth.

Lovell's Library,

Under the title of "LOVELL'S LIBRARY; A WEEKLY PUBLICATION," the undersigned have commenced the publication of all the best works in Current and Standard Literature. It is believed that this issue will be found superior to anything heretofore attempted, especially in the following points: *First*—The type will be larger and the print consquently clearer. *Second*—The size being the popular 12mo, will be found much more pleasant and convenient to handle. *Third*—Each number will have a handsome paper cover; and this, in connection with the size, will make it worthy of preservation.

NUMBERS NOW READY:

	CENTS.
1. **Hyperion**, by Longfellow,	20
2. **Outre-Mer**, by Longfellow	20
3. **The Happy Boy**, by Björnson	10
4. **Arne**, by Björnson	10
5. **Frankenstein**, by Mrs. Shelley	10
6. **The Last of the Mohicans**	20
7. **Clytie**, by Joseph Hatton,	20
8. **The Moonstone**, by Wilkie Collins, Part I	10
9. Do. Part II	10
10. **Oliver Twist**, by Dickens,	20
11. **The Coming Race**; or the New Utopia, by Lord Lytton	10
12. **Leila**; or the Siege of Granada, by Lord Lytton,	10
13. **The Three Spaniards**, by George Walker	20
14. **The Tricks of the Greeks Unveiled**, by Robert Houdin	20
15. **L'Abbe Constantin**, by Ludovic Halévy, author of "La Fille de Mme. Angot," etc.	20
16. **Freckles**, by Rebecca Fergus Redcliff. A new original story	20
17. **The Dark Colleen**, by Mrs. Robert Buchanan,	20
18. **They were Married**, by Walter Besant and James Rice	10
19. **Seekers after God**, by Canon Farrar	20
20. **The Spanish Nun**, by Thos. De Quincey	10
21. **The Green Mountain Boys**, by Judge D. P. Thompson	20
22. **Fleurette**, by Eugene Scribe	20
23. **Second Thoughts**, by Rhoda Broughton	20
24. **The New Magdalen**, by Wilkie Collins	20
25. **Divorce**, by Margaret Lee,	20
26. **Life of Washington**, by Leonard Henley	20
27. **Social Etiquette**, by Mrs. W. A. Saville	15
28. **Single Heart and Double Face**, by Chas. Reade	10
29. **Irene**; or, the Lonely Manor	20
30. **Vice-Versa**, by F. Anstey,	20
31. **Ernest Maltravers**, by Lord Lytton	20

Lovell's Library—CONTINUED.

		CENTS.
32.	The Haunted House and Calderon the Courtier, by Lord Lytton	10
33.	John Halifax, by Miss Mulock	20
34.	800 Leagues on the Amazon, by Jules Verne	10
35.	The Cryptogram, by Jules Verne	10
36.	Life of Marion, by Horry and Weems	20
37.	Paul and Virginia	10
38.	Tale of Two Cities, by Charles Dickens	20
39.	The Hermits, by Rev. Charles Kingsley	20
40.	An Adventure in Thule, and Marriage of Moira Fergus, by Wm. Black	10
41.	A Marriage in High Life, by Octave Feuillet	20
42.	Robin, by Mrs. Parr	20
43.	Two on a Tower, by Thomas Hardy	20
44.	Rasselas, by Samuel Johnson	10
45.	Alice; or the Mysteries, being Part II. of Ernest Maltravers	20
46.	Duke of Kandos, by A. Mathey	20
47.	Baron Munchausen	10
48.	A Princess of Thule, by Wm. Black	20
49.	The Secret Despatch, Grant	20
50.	Early Days of Christianity, by Canon Farrar, D.D., Part I	20
	Do. Part II	20
51.	Vicar of Wakefield, by Oliver Goldsmith	10

		CENTS.
52.	Progress and Poverty, by Henry George	20
53.	The Spy, by J. Fenimore Cooper	20
54.	East Lynne, by Mrs. Henry Wood	20
55.	A Strange Story, by Lord Lytton	20
56.	Adam Bede, by George Eliot, Part I	15
	Do. Part II	15
57.	The Golden Shaft, by Charles Gibbon	20
58.	Portia: or by Passions Rocked, by "The Duchess"	20
59.	Last Days of Pompeii, by Lord Lytton	20
60.	The Two Duchesses, by A. Mathey	20
	Hypatia, by Rev. Charles Kingsley, Part I	15
	Do. Part II	15
	The Vendetta. Tales of Love and Passion, by Honoré de Balzac	20
	Gulliver's Travels, by Dean Swift	20
	Horse Shoe Robinson, by Kennedy, Part I	15
	Do. Part II	15
	Jane Eyre, by Charlotte Brontë	20
	The Wooing O't, by Mrs. Alexander, Part I	15
	Do. Part II	15
	The Admiral's Ward, by Mrs. Alexander	20
	John Wynne's Wives, by C. M. Clay, author of "The Modern Hagar,"	20

www.ingramcontent.com/pod-product-compliance
Lightning Source LLC
Chambersburg PA
CBHW020827190426
43197CB00037B/725